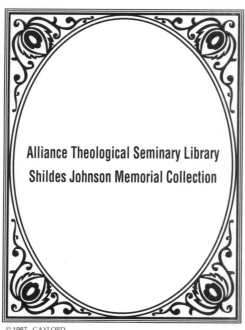

STUDIES IN BIBLICAL THEOLOGY

A series of monographs designed to provide clergy and laymen with the best work in biblical scholarship both in this country and abroad

Advisory Editors:

C. F. D. MOULE, *Lady Margaret's Professor of Divinity in the University of Cambridge*

PETER ACKROYD, *Samuel Davidson Professor of Old Testament Studies, University of London*

JAMES BARR, *Professor of Semitic Languages and Literatures, University of Manchester*

C. F. EVANS, *Professor of New Testament Studies, King's College, London*

FLOYD V. FILSON, *Formerly Professor of New Testament Literature and History, McCormick Theological Seminary, Chicago*

G. ERNEST WRIGHT, *Professor of Old Testament History and Theology at Harvard University*

STUDIES IN BIBLICAL THEOLOGY

Second Series · 16

THE THREAT OF FALSEHOOD

A Study in the Theology of the Book of Jeremiah

THOMAS W. OVERHOLT

SCM PRESS LTD

BLOOMSBURY STREET LONDON

334 01657 6
FIRST PUBLISHED 1970
© SCM PRESS LTD 1970
PRINTED IN GREAT BRITAIN
BY W & J MACKAY & CO LTD, CHATHAM

CONTENTS

PREFACE

THIS study began as a doctoral dissertation done at the University of Chicago under Professors J. Coert Rylaarsdam, Jay A. Wilcoxen, and Gösta W. Ahlström, and it is only fitting that I here express my gratitude to these men, not simply for their help and guidance in this particular project but even more for the stimulus of their teaching and friendship during my time as a student and beyond. I am also in debt to Professors Peter R. Ackroyd and G. Ernest Wright, both of whom read the original manuscript and made many valuable suggestions for its improvement. Finally, I would like to express my appreciation for the efforts of my typist, Mrs Mary Johnson, whose services were placed at my disposal by the Dean of the College.

A shorter version of Chapter II has already appeared in article form as 'Jeremiah 27–29: The Question of False Prophecy', *Journal of the American Academy of Religion,* 35 (1967), pp. 241–49.

Yankton College   THOMAS W. OVERHOLT
South Dakota
March 1970

ABBREVIATIONS

ANET	James B. Pritchard (ed.), *Ancient Near Eastern Texts Relating to the Old Testament* (2nd ed. rev.; Princeton: Princeton University Press, 1955)
BAR I	G. E. Wright and D. N. Freedman (eds.), *The Biblical Archaeologist Reader* (Garden City: Doubleday Anchor, 1961), Vol. I
BAR II	D. N. Freedman and E. F. Campbell, Jr. (eds.), *The Biblical Archaeologist Reader* (Garden City: Doubleday Anchor, 1964), Vol. II
*BHK*³	R. Kittel (ed.), *Biblia Hebraica* (3rd ed. rev.; Stuttgart: Privileg. Württ. Bibelanstalt, 1937)
BJRL	*Bulletin of the John Rylands Library* (Manchester)
BZAW	Beihefte zur Zeitschrift für die Alttestamentliche Wissenschaft
HTR	*Harvard Theological Review* (Cambridge, Mass.)
IB	G. A. Buttrick, *et al.* (eds.), *The Interpreter's Bible* (Nashville: Abingdon, 1952ff.)
IDB	G. A. Buttrick, *et al.* (eds.), *The Interpreter's Dictionary of the Bible* (Nashville: Abingdon, 1962)
JBL	*Journal of Biblical Literature* (Philadelphia)
JBR	*Journal of Bible and Religion* (Wolcott, N.Y.)
JNES	*Journal of Near Eastern Studies* (Chicago)
JTS	*Journal of Theological Studies* (Oxford)
RSV	*The Holy Bible:* Revised Standard Version
SBT	Studies in Biblical Theology (London: SCM Press)
SJT	*Scottish Journal of Theology* (Edinburgh)
SVT	*Supplements to Vetus Testamentum* (Leiden)
ThLZ	*Theologische Literaturzeitung* (Leipzig)
ThZ	*Theologische Zeitschrift* (Basle)
VT	*Vetus Testamentum* (Leiden)
ZAW	*Zeitschrift für die Alttestamentliche Wissenschaft* (Giessen, then Berlin)

I

THE FALSE CONCEPTION OF SECURITY

THE study which follows may be described as an essay on the theology of the Jeremiah tradition, centring on the use in that tradition of the term *šeqer*, commonly translated 'lie, falsehood, deception'. While this noun is fairly frequent within the Old Testament as a whole (111 occurrences), there is such a sudden burst of occurrences in the book of Jeremiah that one immediately suspects that the concept of falsehood had a special significance in the message of that prophet. This is in fact the case, and our study undertakes to show the way in which the prophet took up this concept, extended its connotations, and adopted it as one of the more important terms of his theological vocabulary.

In the book of Jeremiah we encounter the notion of 'falsehood' in connection with three main objects of the prophet's concern: the false sense of security which was preventing the people from responding to Yahweh's call to repentance, the prophetic opponents of Jeremiah ('false prophets'), and the falsehood of idolatry. The first two stand in an especially close relationship to each other, and will be the primary objects of our concern. It is clear that many Judeans of Jeremiah's day were confident that Yahweh would assure the continued existence of their nation in the face of all approaching danger. The presence of the temple in their midst seems to have symbolized for them a guaranteed national security. We may therefore begin our study with an examination of the basis of this confidence and the prophet's reaction to it.

In order to discover Jeremiah's convictions about the people's false sense of security it will be useful to direct our attention to his 'Temple Sermon', for in it the prophet gives a vivid indication of the underlying causes of and factors involved in this attitude. Besides providing us with general information about the conditions under which the message was delivered, Jeremiah 7.1-15

briefly sketches the requirements for continued existence in the
land (vv. 5–7) and then moves on to the basic elements of a
prophetic oracle: an accusation, which describes the people's
actual behaviour (vv. 8–11), and an announcement that Yahweh
will intervene to punish Judah for this behaviour (vv. 12–15).
The latter element of the speech contains an instructive analogy
for Yahweh's intervention in the reference to the fate of Shiloh.
The passage reads:[1]

1, 2 The word which came to Jeremiah from Yahweh saying, Stand
in the gate of Yahweh's house and proclaim there this word
and say, Hear the word of Yahweh, all Judah, (you) who are
3   entering these gates to worship Yahweh. Thus says Yahweh
of hosts the God of Israel, 'Amend your ways and your doings
4   and I will establish you in this place. Do not trust in the false
words saying: "The temple of Yahweh, the temple of Yahweh,
5   the temple of Yahweh these are."[2] For if you surely amend your
6   ways and your doings; and if you surely do justice between a
man and his neighbour; and do not oppress the stranger, orphan,
and widow; nor pour out innocent blood in this place; and do
7   not go after other gods to your own detriment; then I will
establish you in this place, in the land which I gave to your
8   fathers forever. Behold, you trust in false words to no profit.
9   Do you steal, murder, commit adultery, swear falsely, burn
incense to Baal, and go after other gods whom you do not know,
10   and come and stand before me in this house upon which my
name is called and say, "We are delivered!", in order to do
11 all these abominations? Has this house upon which my name is
12 called become a robbers' cave in your eyes? Behold, I myself
have seen it,' says Yahweh. 'For go now to my place which is
in Shiloh, where I established my name at first and see what
13 I did to it because of the evil of my people Israel. And now

---

[1] Some remarks on the relationship of the LXX to the MT are in order.
LXX omits all of v. 1, as well as the details of the place and audience of the
proclamation in v. 2. Beyond this point the texts are remarkably similar, the
only really substantive difference occurring in v. 10, where in place of the
exclamation of the people reported in MT ('We are delivered!', followed by
the prophet's charge) LXX reads the last clause as an assertion by the people
('We have abstained from doing all these abominations!'). In the following
study the MT will be followed.

[2] The most probable explanation of the apparent lack of concord is that
the plural subject reflects the recognition that the temple is a complex of
installations rather than a solitary building. So F. Giesebrecht, *Das Buch
Jeremia* (Göttingen: Vandenhoeck und Ruprecht, 1894), p. 45, and W.
Rudolph, *Jeremia* (3rd ed. rev.; Tübingen: Mohr, 1968), p. 50.

because you have done all these things,' says Yahweh, '– and I
spoke to you persistently and you did not hear, and I called you
14 and you did not answer –, I will do to the house upon which my
name is called in which you trust and to the place which I gave
15 to you and your fathers as I did to Shiloh. I will expel you from
before my face as I expelled all your brothers, all the seed of
Ephraim.'

The general theme of this passage is the continued relationship
of Yahweh to his people, with the specific focus being narrowed
to the problem of their continued existence in the land. The
section begins with a conditional promise of continued existence
in the land (v. 3), and ends with a threat of exile (v. 15). This
emphasis strikes a theme important to both the pre-exilic prophets
and the Deuteronomic history. The prophets were acutely aware
of the fact that the continual sin of the people had placed their
relationship of election in jeopardy (cf. Amos 3.1f.; Jer. 2.4–7,
20–22). One must also remember that in the age during which
both Jeremiah and the Deuteronomists operated the uncertain
status of the people's continued existence in the land was a major
theme for historical reasons: Judah was approaching (or, in the
case of the final editing of the Deuteronomic history, had reached)
the end of her independent political existence. This means that
during the whole period of Jeremiah's activity the problem of
explaining the people's apparent feeling of security is related to a
basic political question: In the face of growing Babylonian power
and increasing Egyptian weakness (certainly both would have
been evident after 605), what could have possessed first Jehoiakim
and then Zedekiah to adopt their disastrous policies of revolt
against Babylon? We can, of course, assume that many factors
were involved: the temporary setback suffered by Nebuchadnezzar in 601, the pro-Egyptian sentiments of some of the nobility,
and perhaps others as well. In what follows I will suggest that a
false notion of what it meant to be a chosen people (mirrored
already in Amos 3.1f.) was a factor of crucial importance.

Despite the gathering political storm, many of the prophet's
contemporaries found comfort in the fact that the 'temple of
Yahweh' stood in their midst. The question is how the temple
could function as a symbol of the people's confidence that Yahweh would guarantee their national security. The answer would
seem to be that the roots of this confidence sink deep into the soil

of Israel's two great covenant traditions, both of which were connected with the temple cultus: Sinai (bound up, we must remember, with the Pentateuchal promise of the land) and David (the guarantee of a continuing monarchy).[3] The interventions of Yahweh in history which form the background of these two covenants were 'constitutive for Israel', so that we can in fact view them as two election traditions which were the 'foundation' for all subsequent thought about the relationship between Yahweh and his people.[4] The crucial aspect of Yahweh's presence with his people is felt to be what he *does* with them. The real danger, therefore, is that they will take his past actions on their behalf (as mirrored in these two election traditions) as *normative* for all his future dealings with them.

It is possible to focus even more specifically on the history which lies behind the Temple Sermon. Commentators have generally recognized the connection between 7.1–15 and ch. 26, usually considering the former to be a preservation (or at least a report) of the speech which is only summarized in the course of the narrative of ch. 26.[5] The date given in 26.1 (probably 608)[6]

[3] On the connection between royal ideology and the temple cultus cf. W. F. Albright, *Archaeology and the Religion of Israel* (4th ed. rev.; Baltimore: Johns Hopkins Press, 1956), pp. 130–75; H. Ringgren, *Israelite Religion,* trans. David E. Green (London: SPCK, and Philadelphia: Fortress Press, 1966), pp. 151–238; H. J. Kraus, *Psalmen* (Neukirchen: Moers, 1960), II, 'Exkurs 6: Königtum und Kultus in Jerusalem', pp. 879–83, and *Worship in Israel,* trans. G. Buswell (Oxford: Blackwell, and Richmond, Va.: John Knox Press, 1966), pp. 179–238; and G. W. Ahlström, *Aspects of Syncretism in Israelite Religion* (Lund: Gleerup, 1963), pp. 34–45. On the Sinai covenant cf. S. Mowinckel, *Le Décalogue* (Paris: Librairie Felix Alcan, 1927), especially pp. 129–38, 156ff.; G. von Rad, 'The Problem of the Hexateuch' (especially sections 4–6), *The Problem of the Hexateuch and Other Essays,* trans. E. E. Trueman Dickens (Edinburgh: Oliver and Boyd, 1966), pp. 20–40.

[4] G. von Rad, *Old Testament Theology,* trans. D. M. G. Stalker (Edinburgh: Oliver and Boyd, and New York: Harper and Row, 1962–65), I, p. 255 (cited henceforth as *Theology* I, II).

[5] J. G. Eichhorn, *Die hebraischen Propheten* (Göttingen: Vandenhoeck und Ruprecht, 1819), II; F. Hitzig, *Der Prophet Jeremia* (Leipzig: Weidmannsche Buchhandlung, 1841), who thinks that the same oracle was repeated on two different occasions; K. H. Graf, *Der Prophet Jeremia erklärt* (Leipzig: T. O. Weigel, 1862); C. von Orelli, *The Prophecies of Jeremiah,* trans. J. S. Banks (Edinburgh: T. & T. Clark, 1889); F. Giesebrecht, *ad loc.,* who considers ch. 7 to be Baruch's recapitulation of the original speech; B. Duhm, *Das Buch Jeremia* (Tübingen: J. C. B. Mohr, 1901), who thinks 7.3–15 reflects an actual speech, though it is much worked over by post-exilic editors; C. H. Cornill, *Das Buch Jeremia erklärt* (Leipzig: C. H. Tauchnitz, 1905); S. R. Driver, *The Book of the Prophet Jeremiah* (London: Hodder and Stoughton, and New York:

is thus accepted for both. Within the very recent past a great king has been killed and another deposed. Egypt was still asserting her power in Palestine, but the spectre of Neo-Babylonian domination loomed large on the horizon.

The time was thus one of severe political and theological insecurity. The reign of Josiah had been a period of growing optimism in both of these spheres. Coming to the throne at a time of increasing Assyrian weakness, Josiah seems to have gradually asserted Judah's independence from that once-mighty world power. It is likely that he 'aspired to restore the empire of David',[7] and he apparently had some success in this, for we hear of his pressing his reforms beyond the borders of Judah into the region of Samaria (II Kings 23.19). Megiddo, where he met Neco and where he apparently had freedom of movement, was the capital of the Assyrian province of Galilee. The reform of 621 BC should be seen both as another indication of growing political independence from Assyria and as a focal point for a resurgence of religious optimism, and R. Davidson has pointed out that it was precisely this optimism which became one of the basic points of contention between Jeremiah and the people.[8] But now Josiah was suddenly dead and his son Jehoahaz, whom the people had wanted to be

---

Scribner, 1906); P. Volz, *Der Prophet Jeremia* (Leipzig: A. Deichert, 1922); A. Weiser, *Der Prophet Jeremia* (4th ed. rev.; Göttingen: Vandenhoeck und Ruprecht, 1960), and finally, three other recent commentators, all of whom consider ch. 7 as we have it a product of Deuteronomic editing: E. A. Leslie, *Jeremiah* (New York: Abingdon, 1954); W. Rudolph, *ad loc.*; J. P. Hyatt, *IB* V.

[6] Mowinckel assumes that the phrase 'in the beginning of the reign of . . .' (Jer. 26.1) places the Temple Sermon at the time of Jehoiakim's enthronement (he cites the use of an identical Assyrian phrase in this context). The speech thus '. . . takes as its starting point precisely the main thoughts of the festival: the complete confidence of the people in the promises of Yahweh with regard to the existence and importance of the temple. The basis of this becomes still clearer and the idea still more distinct if we consider it against the background of the thought in Ps. 93.5: the faith in the trustworthy promises guaranteed by the re-consecrated temple.' *The Psalms in Israel's Worship*, trans. D. Ap-Thomas (Oxford: Blackwell, and Nashville: Abingdon, 1962), I, p. 129.

[7] M. Noth, *The History of Israel*, rev. trans. (London: A. and C. Black, 1960), p. 273. J. Bright, *A History of Israel* (Philadelphia: Westminster, and London: SCM Press, 1959), p. 298, describes Josiah's reform as 'a facet of resurgent nationalism'.

[8] R. Davidson, 'Orthodoxy and the Prophetic Word: A Study in the Relationship between Jeremiah and Deuteronomy', *VT* 14 (1964), pp. 408–12.

king, deposed by Pharaoh Neco and replaced by Jehoiakim. Yahweh had apparently responded negatively to widespread reform and obedience, and this surprising turn of events seems to have rendered the fact of Josiah's death so embarrassing to the basic presuppositions of the prophets and the Deuteronomic school regarding a theology of history that we have in the Old Testament materials something that amounts to a 'conspiracy of silence' about this tragic occurrence.[9]

As G. E. Wright phrases it, the problem which confronted the people of Judah in this historical situation can be summed up in the question of whether all Yahweh's promises in the reform of Josiah had been in vain. Was this 'the answer of God to reform and obedience'?[10] Old covenant promises had thus come into apparent conflict with current events, and the temple became a focal point in a discussion of the bases of national security.

Verse 2 sets the stage, indicating that the speech which follows is addressed to those who are entering the temple to worship there. The addressees conceived of themselves as 'worshippers' of Yahweh, entitled to all the benefits attending their status as the elect of God.[11] The burden of Jeremiah's message, however, is that they will not partake of these benefits, for the relationship of election is near the breaking point. Paul Volz has expressed the dominant theme of this message as follows:

Through the speech of Jeremiah there moves as a leitmotif the question: What gives security?, for the people, intimidated by the immediately preceding political events, sought security. The leaders say: the temple, the sacrifices are our protection; the people believe it; Jeremiah says: the only protection, the sole surety of the nation and personal welfare is a moral life: *you* must protect the temple, it is not able to protect you.[12]

Wright has noted that from this point on the passage is cast in a form similar to that of a legal brief, with vv. 3–4 functioning as a

---

[9] Cf. S. B. Frost, 'The Death of Josiah: A Conspiracy of Silence', *JBL* 87 (1968), pp. 369–82.

[10] 'Security and Faith: An Exposition of Jeremiah 7.1–15', in *The Rule of God: Essays in Biblical Theology* (Garden City, N.Y.: Doubleday, 1960), p. 82.

[11] Cf. G. Fohrer, 'Jeremias Tempelwort 7.1–15', *ThZ* 5 (1949), p. 402.

[12] Volz, *ad loc*. His statement has a marked influence on later commentators (cf. Rudolph and Hyatt) and seems to be essentially correct, although one may wish to differ with his lopsided stress on the ethical.

statement of Yahweh's case.[13] The prophet begins with an exhortation to the people to 'amend' their ways in order that they may continue their existence 'in this place'. The notion that repentance will result in Yahweh's establishing them 'in this place' is reiterated in v. 7, where the 'place' is specifically identified as 'the land which I gave to your fathers for ever and ever'. In v. 14 the 'house' and 'place' are mentioned together as objects of Yahweh's punishment, the latter being described as something which has been given 'to you and your fathers'.

Within the Old Testament both the land and the kingdom are entities which are given or established 'forever'. As to the former, it is well to remember that concern with the giving of the promised land is not simply Deuteronomic, but is the goal of the *Heilsgeschichte* reflected in Deuteronomy 26.5–9 and the whole Hexateuch. The promise and its eventual fulfilment form a recurring theme which in some sense gives cohesion to the material beginning with the patriarchs and ending with the conquest (cf. Gen. 13.15, J; 17.8 and 48.4, P; Josh. 14.9).[14] With regard to the latter, Psalm 89 shows us how central the establishment of the dynasty 'forever' (v. 5) was to the covenant with David. Yahweh has willed the kingship (David is his 'chosen one', v. 4) and will preserve it. Infraction of his *tōrâ* will be punished, but the covenant will not be abrogated. 'Through the covenant the king is obliged to keep Yahweh's *tōrâ*, v. 31, and has to communicate the *tōrâ* to the people. Further, the covenant signifies that the continuation of the people is guaranteed through the royal family which was chosen by God.'[15] The covenant with David thus becomes a further confirmation of Yahweh's enduring promise to establish his people in the land.[16] Yet Jeremiah knows that the people's rebellion is also 'from forever' (2.20), a long-established habit which they are now powerless to break (2.22; 13.23). The existence of the people is characterized by a tension between covenant and apostasy.

It has long been recognized that the assumption reflected in 7.4 which forms the basis of the people's 'trust' is that Yahweh

[13] *Op. cit.*, p. 84.
[14] Cf. von Rad, *Theology* I, pp. 167–70, 296–305.
[15] G. W. Ahlström, *Psalm 89* (Lund: G. W. K. Gleerups Forlag, 1959), p. 52.
[16] II Sam. 7.13, 16; 23.5; I Kings 9.5; Ps. 89.2–4, 28–37; cf. also P. S. Minear, 'Promise', *IDB* 3 (K–Q), pp. 893–95, and Ps. 105.7–11, where establishment in the land is secured by an everlasting covenant.

would under no circumstances allow his temple to be destroyed.[17] But Jeremiah considers this confidence to be misplaced, and pictures the people as trusting in 'the words of the lie' (vv. 4, 8). Over a century ago F. Hitzig recognized that this phrase does not simply refer to the words of false prophets, but rather to deceitful objects of thought which allow the people to sleep securely.[18] Verse 4 makes the simple identification of 'lying words' with the exclamation 'This is the temple of Yahweh.' The remainder of the passage is concerned with pointing out what it means to utter such a 'lie' (vv. 5–11) and why it is to be considered a 'lie' (vv. 12–15).[19]

Verses 5–7 now set out the stipulations of the covenant in the form of a conditional sentence which elaborates on v. 3 by showing both what will be involved in the people's amending their ways and what the result of such repentance will be. The use of *'im* with the imperfect indicates that the condition is considered capable of fulfilment.[20] The content of the act of repentance is summed up in four general requirements (introduced by a second 'if'):

1. The requirement to 'do justice between a man and his neighbour'. The term *mišpaṭ* is closely connected with the covenant stipulations (Ex. 21.1), and so the phrase is most often used in connection with the doing of Yahweh's ordinances. The reference may simply be to the exercising of an actual legal precedent or rule

---

[17] Cf. Eichhorn, Rudolph, Fohrer. Several commentators tie this belief either wholly or in part to the events of 701, e.g., von Orelli, Giesebrecht, Volz, and Weiser. 'The estimation of that building as the palace of Yahweh is the basis of the superstitious confidence: Yahweh's temple cannot perish, as the attack of Sennacherib in the time of Hezekiah had proven.' Giesebrecht, *op. cit.,* p. 45.

[18] *Op. cit.,* p. 62; on the problem of the nature and content of false prophecy, cf. Chapter II below.

[19] Notice should be taken of J. Hermann's comments on the triple repetition of words and phrases in Jer. 7.4; 22.29, and Ezek. 21.32 (Isa. 6.3 is excluded, since it is a liturgical formula and thus of a different nature than these passages). Though the usual interpretation of these passages (i.e., repetition for the sake of emphasis) is adequate, the possibility also exists that we see reflected here the form of certain Babylonian exorcisms, which began with the same kind of triple repetition. 'Zu Jeremia 22.29; 7.4', *ZAW* 62 (1950), 321f. Though its roots sink deep into the basic religious traditions of the people, trust in the temple is perhaps not without its magical aspect.

[20] *Gesenius' Hebrew Grammar,* rev. by E. Kautzsch, trans. A. E. Cowley (Oxford: The Clarendon Press, 1910), paragraph 159b and 1; cf. G. Brockelmann, *Hebräische Syntax* (Verlag der Buchhandlung des Erziehungsvereins Neukirchen Kreis Moers, 1956), paragraphs 164, 166.

(e.g., Ex. 21.9, 31), or it may constitute a general statement of the necessity of men to be obedient to these ordinances (e.g., Lev. 18.4). The action of 'doing justice' is one which is specifically required of the king,[21] whose relationship with Yahweh is conditional upon his doing of Yahweh's ordinances (I Kings 6.12; 11.33). Thus the connotation of the phrase 'do justice' is highly legal-ethical, even in the case of the king (where this aspect of his commission is stressed). The phrase itself could become a prophetic catch-word (cf. Micah 6.8). The use of the noun *mišpaṭ* in Jeremiah corresponds to these observations about the phrase 'do justice'. In connection with human action the reference is, on the one hand, to the *mišpaṭ* of Yahweh which the people do not know or do (5.1, 4f., 28; 8.7), and, on the other, to the social justice which the king must (21.12; 22.3, 13, 15) or will (23.5; 33.15) do.

2. The requirement not to oppress the widow and orphan. This is a phrase not often found verbatim in the prophets (cf. Isa. 1.17, Jer. 22.3), but E. Hammershaimb has shown that when viewed in its proper context (the problem of legal protection for the unjustly oppressed) prophetic parallels are frequent.[22] This command is also important outside the prophets in passages like Ex. 22.21; Deut. 10.18 and 24.17; and Ps. 68.6, where it is used as a title for Yahweh.

3. The requirement not to spill 'innocent blood'. This stipulation is tied up with the concept of bloodguilt, which is incurred by the slaying of one who does not deserve to die (both killing in self-defence and the judicial execution of criminals are exempted; cf. Ex. 22.1f.; Lev. 20.9).[23] One of the functions of the king is to guard against the shedding of innocent blood (Jer. 22.3, 17),[24] and when he does not fulfil this function the whole society reaches the point where it may fairly be characterized as a group which thrives on shedding the life-blood of the innocent poor (Jer. 2.34). The presence of bloodguilt within a group has serious implications, its

[21] Cf. II Sam. 8.15 (= I Chr. 18.14); I Kings 10.9. Relevant here is Buber's idea that the Messiah is but a king 'who fulfills the function assigned to him at his anointing', *The Prophetic Faith,* trans. C. Witton-Davies (New York: Harper and Row, 1960), pp. 144, 153.

[22] 'On the Ethics of the Old Testament Prophets', *SVT* 7 (1960), pp. 75–101; see, for example, Amos 2.6f.; 4.1; Micah 3.1f.; 6.6–8.

[23] Cf. M. Greenberg, 'Bloodguilt', *IDB* 1 (A–D), pp. 449f.

[24] Only the wicked ruler shed innocent blood: II Kings 21.16 (Manasseh), Ps. 94.20f.

consequences ending to the whole community. II Kings 24.4, for example, attributes Nebuchadnezzar's destruction of Jerusalem to Manasseh's sins and bloodguilt (cf. also Jer. 26.15, Joel 4.19, and Jonah 1.14).

At this point notice should be taken of the close correspondence between these three requirements and the demands made of the king in Jeremiah 22.3. The latter correspond closely to the major emphases of the king's commission as reflected, for example, in Psalm 72.[25]

4. The prohibition against going after 'other gods'. The occurrences of the phrase 'other gods' in Jeremiah leave little doubt that these deities were worshipped by the people, who are described as, among other things, going after them (7.6, 9; 11.10; 13.10; 16.11; 25.6; 35.15), burning incense to them (1.16; 19.4; 44.5, 8, 15), and offering libations to them (7.18; 19.13; 32.29). 7.6. says that they do this 'to their own detriment', a threat which several passages interpret in terms of the destruction and subsequent exile of Judah (cf. 1.15f.; 16.10–13; 25.6, 8–11). In this exile the people really will be separated from Yahweh's help and reduced to serving 'other gods' (16.13; cf. I Sam. 26.19). This phrase is also common in the Deuteronomic History (38 occurrences in Deut. through II Kings), where it is often connected with the conditional nature of continued residence in the land (e.g., Josh. 23.16). But we should not jump to the conclusion that the problem reflected by it is a late one in Israelite religious history or that the phrase is 'Deuteronomic'. There are a number of examples of earlier occurrences, among them Ex. 20.3 and Deut. 5.7 (the Decalogue), Ex. 23.13 (part of the legislation of the Book of the Covenant), I Samuel 26.19 (David's complaint that he is a fugitive because of men who say, 'Go, serve other gods'), and Hosea 3.1 (of the people's apostasy). The attitude of the people toward these gods is not constant. Sometimes in a crisis a reversion to the exclusive worship of Yahweh seems to have occurred (e.g., Jer. 14.19-22), yet one cannot deny either the pervasiveness of the worship of 'other gods' or the fact that this worship was actually

---

[25] Ps. 72 emphasizes the king's obligation to defend the cause of the poor and oppressed, of him who has no helper (note the use of the noun *mišpaṭ* in v. 2 and of *dām* in v. 14). In this respect 7.9f., addressed to the people, and 22.3, addressed to the king, at several points phrase this obligation in identical terms (' "do" justice', 'alien, fatherless, and widow', 'you shall not shed innocent blood in this place').

thought to be effective: the gods were expected to render concrete assistance (11.9-13; cf. 2.26-29).

The result of fulfilling these conditions, which we have seen exhibit connections with both the Sinai and Davidic covenants, is the continued existence of the nation in the promised land (v. 7). A. Weiser in particular stresses the connection of this passage with the covenant. Verses 3b–8 refer, he says, to the possession of the land at the beginning and the end, and contain a statement of 'the basic religious and social-ethical demands of the covenant'. The repetition of the warning against false trust (vv. 4, 8) highlights the true reliability of the covenant promise, while at the same time the passage as a whole makes the point that 'the covenant salvation remains bound to the covenant demand'.[26]

Verses 8–11 form a prophetic accusation directed against the actual behaviour of the people. In the opening phrase – 'you are trusting in the words of the lie' – we have an almost exact parallel to v. 4a, and one should notice here the larger parallelism within the passage as a whole. Verse 3 calls the people to repentance as a condition for their remaining in the land, and v. 4 accuses them of trusting in a lie ('this is the temple of Yahweh'). Verses 5–7 repeat the elements of v. 3, adding to them a statement suggesting the proper nature of the called-for repentance, while vv. 8–11 repeat the accusation that the people are trusting in a lie and make it more specific by detailing some of their actual socio-religious activities as well as the precise nature of their trust in the temple ('we are delivered!'). Verses 5–11 thus constitute a parallel to, as well as a more detailed development of, vv. 3–4, spelling out what it means to utter the lying words 'this is the temple of Yahweh.' In terms of vv. 8–11 the confidence displayed in this phrase indicates two basic things about the people's attitude:

1. It indicates, first of all, that the people had developed an easy attitude toward the covenant regulations. The list of infractions found in v. 9 is brief, but specific: the people are said to be guilty of theft, murder, adultery, swearing falsely, burning incense to Baal, and going after other gods. The picture which this accusation sketches of the prophet's assessment of the type of behaviour which is characteristic of his audience is relatively unambiguous, although there may be room for some latitude of connotations in

[26] Weiser, *ad loc.*

the matter of false swearing. The legal notion of false witnesses in
court actions is the first thing which comes to mind, but given the
nature of the charges made later in the verse the term might also be
taken to refer to an oath taken in the name of another god (cf.
12.16). We might even interpret the phrase as referring to the
protestations of a sinful people as they present themselves in the
temple as legitimate and worthy worshippers of Yahweh (v. 2).
Perhaps all these things are involved.

We must assume that behind the specific charge in v. 9 there
lies some model of what constitutes proper obedience to Yahweh.
We thus come face to face with the problem of the norm used by
the prophets in their condemnation of the people's behaviour.
Currently we are coming to recognize more and more the extent
to which the prophets stood as heirs to the religious traditions of
their people. R. E. Clements has commented that recent studies in
the covenant, cult, and law have helped to bring into focus their
'primary role as the messengers of Yahweh who were concerned
with the covenant relationship between Yahweh and Israel'.[27]
They did not preach a new code of ethics or develop a new legal
system, but rather drew attention to 'a crisis in the history of the
covenant' caused by the nation's persistent sin.[28] Seen in the light
of the whole history of Israel's religion, the significance of the
canonical prophets thus lies in their part in 'maintaining and inter-
preting the Yahwistic tradition through the years of crisis. Their
unique contribution to Israel's faith was to have actualized the
covenant tradition in the days of its obscurity and loss.'[29]

If the term 'covenant' itself is infrequent in the recorded
utterances of most of the pre-exilic prophets, this is understandable for as J. Lindblom points out, '. . . the judicial character of
this idea led the people to make claims on their God as of right
and to cherish ambiguous dreams of a supposedly inevitable
glorious future. It was a primary task of the pre-exilic prophets to
combat such false illusions. To them the essential was not the

[27] *Prophecy and Covenant* (SBT, First Series, 43, 1965), p. 25.
[28] *Ibid.,* p. 79.
[29] *Ibid.,* p. 124. Cf. also N. W. Porteous, 'The Prophets and the Problem of
Continuity', *Israel's Prophetic Heritage,* ed. B. W. Anderson and W. Harrelson
(New York: Harper, and London: SCM Press, 1962), pp. 11–25; P. R.
Ackroyd, *Continuity* (Oxford: Blackwell, 1962), p. 19; G. von Rad, *Theology,*
II, p. 130 and often; W. Zimmerli, *The Law and the Prophets* (New York:
Harper and Row, 1967).

claim of the people on Yahweh, but Yahweh's claim on Israel in virtue of election.[30] Yet their concern was decidedly with Yahweh's will and the ancient customs and statutes of the covenant. One might say that 'the prophets did not need to mention the covenant so much, as they lived completely within it, in their points of view, in their preaching'.[31]

Work has also been done in the area of form criticism to demonstrate the basis of the connection of the prophetic preaching with the covenant. H. B. Huffmon, for example, has dealt with the problem raised by certain 'lawsuit' oracles in which an appeal is made to the natural elements (heaven, earth, etc.; cf. Isa. 1.2f., Jer. 2.4–13), turning to the Hittite international treaties in which gods and natural elements stand as witnesses for a solution. He recognized that the appeal to these elements stands in lawsuits in which Israel is being indicted for breach of her covenant with Yahweh, assuming that though the precise function of these witnesses was unclear the form went back ultimately to some 'actual court procedure'.[32] E. von Waldow has carried this line of inquiry further, attempting to show that while the form of certain prophetic speeches of judgment goes back to profane legal procedure, their content (the identity of the judge and claimant) derives from the covenant tradition.[33] G. E. Wright has also stressed what he considers to be primarily the political function of the prophets in announcing Yahweh's 'covenant lawsuit' (*rîb*) against the people.[34]

In Jeremiah the term *berîth* occurs with some frequency, but always in one of two contexts: either references to the Sinai covenant in which the point of emphasis is that the people have been guilty of infractions of its stipulations and will therefore be

---

[30] J. Lindblom, *Prophecy in Ancient Israel* (Oxford: Blackwell, 1962), p. 329. H.-J. Kraus has pointed out that 'even in the vegetation cult' any attempt to exert power over the god through the performing of sacrifice, etc. is a prostitution of the real meaning of the divine-human relationship; *Worship in Israel*, p. 124.

[31] A. S. Kapelrud, 'The Role of the Cult in Old Israel', *The Bible in Modern Scholarship*, ed. J. P. Hyatt (Nashville: Abingdon, 1965), p. 55.

[32] 'The Covenant Lawsuit in the Prophets', *JBL* 78 (1959), pp. 285–95.

[33] *Der Traditionsgeschichtliche Hintergrund der prophetischen Gerichtsreden*, BZAW 85 (1963), especially pp. 12–25.

[34] Cf., 'The Lawsuit of God: A Form-Critical Study of Deuteronomy 32', *Israel's Prophetic Heritage*, pp. 26–67, and 'The Nations in Hebrew Prophecy', *Encounter* 26 (1965), pp. 225–37.

punished at the hands of Yahweh (11.2, 3, 6, 8, 10;[35] 34.8, 10, 13, 15, 18; as well as 22.9 and, by implication, 14.21), or references to a 'new' or reaffirmed covenant which will accompany Yahweh's restoration of the nation (31.31, 32, 33; 32.40; 33.20, 21, 25; 50.5; cf. also 3.16). For Jeremiah the people have broken the covenant, and it is clear that 7.9 does actually reflect commandments 1–2 and 6–9 of the Decalogue, although the order in which these appear is somewhat different from that in Ex. 20.[36] This fact has led most commentators to assume that Jeremiah is here utilizing the Decalogue, though it is true that he treats it with considerable prophetic freedom.[37] Hosea 4.1–6 is another example of a prophetic appeal to such a list of commandments. Since the priests had mismanaged their important function of transmitting Yahweh's torah, the great prophets appear at times to have taken this function upon themselves.[38]

But the problem of the norm of prophetic judgment is too complex to be resolved by simply noting the similarity of these passages to the Decalogue.[39] It could be noted that E. Hammer-

---

[35] J. W. Miller has dealt with this passage in his study *Das Verhältnis Jeremias und Hesekiels sprachlich und theologisch Untersucht* (Aussen: Van Gorcum, 1955). Miller's thesis is that in collecting into a roll his oracles of 23 years (cf. Jer. 36) the prophet consciously gave them a literary form based on the sequence of the covenant ceremony (as seen in Deut. and Ex. 19ff.). Thus Jer. 11.1–8 corresponds to Deut. 27.14–26, the blessing and curse section of the ceremony, while vv. 9–14 correspond to Deut. 26.17–19, the obligation of the covenant; pp. 42ff. The passage itself yields the following information: the covenant referred to is that of Sinai (vv. 4, 7), the emphasis is upon the curse connected with the covenant (v. 3), the coming destruction is because both the people and their fathers have broken the covenant (v. 11), the main charge is that they have worshipped other gods (vv. 10, 12f., 17).

[36] Using the sequence of the commandments in Ex. 20/Deut. 5 as the basis of enumeration, the order in Jer. 7.9 is as follows: 8, 6, 7, 9, 2, 1. In Hos. 4.2 it is: 3, 6, 8, 7.

[37] E.g., Hitzig, Graf, von Orelli, Giesebrecht, Duhm, Volz, Rudolph, Weiser, Hyatt, Wright and Fohrer; on this see especially W. Eichrodt, 'The Right Interpretation of the Old Testament: A Study of Jeremiah 7.1–15', *Theology Today* 7 (1950–51), pp. 15–25.

[38] Cf. J. Lindblom, *op. cit.*, pp. 156f., 347; H. W. Wolff, *Dodekapropheten* 1: *Hosea* (Neukirchen: Neukirchener Verlag, 1961), pp. 90ff.

[39] This is essentially the solution offered by E. J. Smith, who says: 'The sins censured by Jeremias throughout his preaching are nothing else but offenses against the Decalogue.' 'The Decalogue in the Preaching of Jeremias', *CBQ* 4 (1942), p. 201. Smith's assumption, of course, is that the Decalogue not only comes from Moses, but also carries great weight with the people and would therefore be an effective basis for the prophet's appeal. Apart from this assumption, it seems to me that the method by which he identifies

shaimb has even shown that the basis of their ethical teaching cannot always be thought of as uniquely Israelite.⁴⁰ Perhaps all we should conclude is that behind the ethical preaching of the prophets there lies a traditional body of legal stipulations of complex origin which they consider the people obliged to obey if they are to maintain their relationship to Yahweh. This means that even when it is not expressly stated these stipulations are treated as covenant obligations.⁴¹

The focal point of all this is the temple which is 'called by Yahweh's name' (7, 10, 11, 14), that is, which Yahweh has publicly proclaimed as his sanctuary. (K. Galling has noted the connection of this formula with the ancient Near Eastern practice of public, oral proclamation of the transfer of commercial property.⁴²) Yahweh has 'allowed' the temple 'to be known by his name', and therefore to serve as a 'bridge' over the gap which existed 'between the distant heavenly God and the desire for and knowledge of his nearness.'⁴³ It is here that he confronts his people with a demand that they be obedient to his will (vv. 5–9). But Jeremiah makes it immediately clear that the people have failed to respond

---

supposed quotations of the Decalogue in Jeremiah's preaching is rather questionable. For example, the mere presence of the word *šqr* is often enough to assign a particular passage to the eighth commandment (false witness). While this identification seems possible in 7.9, it is scarcely even probable in 3.23 or in those passages where the subject being dealt with is false prophecy (certainly a phenomenon much more complex than what the Decalogue meant by 'false witness'; 27.14–16; 28.15; 29.9, 21 are all cited by Smith as reflecting the eighth commandment).

⁴⁰ *Op. cit.* (See n. 22 above).
⁴¹ Cf. also N. W. Porteous, 'The Basis of the Ethical Teaching of the Prophets', *Studies in Old Testament Prophecy*, ed. H. H. Rowley (Edinburgh: T. & T. Clark, 1946), pp. 143–56. For Porteous the two foci of the prophetic ethic are (most importantly) the Mosaic tradition and certain ethical notions common in the ancient Near East. He accepts the idea that both prophet and priest were 'concerned with the task of preserving and handing on the tradition', with 'inculcating a known morality', p. 149. The prophets are not distinguished by the uniqueness of what they said, but by the compelling conviction with which they said it. J. P. Hyatt seems to me to make too much of the supposed conflict between the cultic written torah of the priests and the ethical, Mosaic torah of the prophets; cf. 'Torah in the Book of Jeremiah', *JBL* 60 (1941), pp. 381–96.
⁴² 'Die Ausrufung des Namens als Rechtsakt in Israel', *ThLZ* 81 (1956), pp. 65–70. Cf. the Middle Assyrian laws translated by T. J. Meek, *ANET*, especially p. 185.
⁴³ G. E. Wright, 'The Temple in Palestine-Syria', *BAR* I, p. 182.

to that demand. They have instead made a claim of their own: 'No matter what we do we are secure!' The prophet's polemic is not to be viewed as simply a depreciation of the cultus in favour of a more ethically-oriented religion. For the people's behaviour regarding the temple is but a symptom of a more fundamental theological error.

2. The second thing it means to utter the lying words 'this is the temple of Yahweh' is that the people have an easy attitude about the certainty of Yahweh's protection. This is expressed in v. 10 by the simple exclamation, 'We are delivered!' To what does this cry refer?

An interpretation of this exclamation depends upon our understanding of the verb *nṣl*, a term which is fairly common in the Old Testament literature in the sense of 'snatch away, rescue, deliver'. Most frequently it is said that God delivers someone from the peril of a threatening enemy (e.g., Judg. 8.34), although sometimes the reference is simply to the leader who brings about military deliverance (e.g., Judg. 9.17, I Sam. 14.48).

An examination of several passages containing clusters of occurrences of the verb yields the same impression: the basic connotation of *nṣl* is that of deliverance from physical peril. In the various versions of the Isaiah narratives (Isa. 36f.; II Kings 18f.; II Chron. 32) the verb occurs 27 times altogether. Here the basic idea, enunciated by the Rabshakeh, is that neither Hezekiah nor Yahweh nor the gods of the nations have been able (or will be able) to deliver a besieged people from the hands of the Assyrian king. Ex. 18.4–10 (4 occurrences) speaks of Yahweh as the deliverer of Moses (from the sword of Pharaoh) and his people (from bondage). Ezek. 14.14–20 (6 occurrences) asserts that when Yahweh stretches out his hand against a sinful land even men like Noah, David, and Job are powerless to deliver anyone. Only they themselves will be delivered.

The connotation is essentially the same in several passages where cultic elements are explicitly present. I Samuel 4 describes how the ark was brought from Shiloh to the Israelite camp in hope that its presence would turn the tide of the battle in their favour. The initial reaction of the Philistines to its arrival is reported to have been one of panic: 'Who can deliver us from the power of these mighty gods? These are the gods who smote the Egyptians . . .' (v. 8). Deliverance is equated with success in battle against a powerful enemy. Later in the same book the account of Samuel's farewell address has the prophet exhorting the people to be obedient to Yahweh and not to turn aside after 'vain things which cannot profit or deliver' (12.21). By contrast, the context stresses Yahweh's 'saving deeds' (*ṣid̠eqôth*, v. 7), the reference being to his military accomplishments on behalf of his people, cf. vv. 8, 11). II Kings 17.35–39 is also interesting, since it makes an explicit connection between the term and Yahweh's covenant. The narrative context tells of the spread of Yahwism among new inhabitants of Israel after the Assyrian deportation of the population in 721. Yahweh, the God who had accomplished the exodus, made a covenant with these people and commanded that they be obedient to its ordinances. They were not to fear other gods, but Yahweh alone, who would deliver them out of the hands of their enemies (v. 39).

It is also worth mentioning that *nṣl* occurs once (Num. 35.25) in connection with the regulations regarding manslaughter and the cities of refuge (cf. vv. 9–34). In Israel one could gain temporary refuge at an altar of Yahweh (I Kings 1.50–53; 2.28–34), but provision was also made for long-term protection of those guilty of manslaughter. The principle involved was that the chance manslayer was permitted to remain safe in one of the cities of refuge, while he who was guilty of murder must be turned over to the avenger of blood (this is the excuse which justified the slaying of Joab even as he clung to the altar, I Kings 2.28–34). Numbers 35 assigns the task of determining guilt or innocence to the 'congregation', whose task it is to 'rescue' (v. 25) the unintentional manslayer from the avenger and restore him to the city of refuge.[44]

What did the people have in mind when they stood in the temple and uttered the words 'We are delivered'? Viewing the evidence cited above in light of the observation that the main issue in the Temple Sermon as a whole is whether the people are to be allowed to remain in their land (vv. 3, 7, 14f.), it seems only natural to assume that uppermost in their consciousness was the confidence that in a time of political instability Yahweh would

---

44 Cf. M. Greenberg, 'City of Refuge', *IDB* 1 (A–D), pp. 638f.; idem, 'The Biblical Conception of Asylum', *JBL* 78 (1959), pp. 125–32; R. de Vaux, *Ancient Israel*, trans. J. McHugh (New York: McGraw-Hill, and London: Darton, Longman and Todd, 1961), pp. 160–63; J. Gray, *I & II Kings* (London: SCM Press, and Philadelphia: Westminster, 1963), pp. 94, 107.

guarantee the safety of their national state. One gets the distinct impression that the message these men were conveying was simply this: Yahweh is our God, and come what may he will never allow us, who come here and worship in his temple, to be completely overcome. Jeremiah saw the situation differently, and the nature of his insight (which we have until now been speaking of by reference to the covenant traditions) can be expressed very well in the language of the law of the manslayer (such expression is consistent with part of the demand he makes in v. 6 and the charge in v. 9): The right to refuge and safety can only be legitimately claimed by the innocent. Thus, just as the community must weed out the guilty parties who falsely claim the right of refuge and deliver them over to justice, so Yahweh must deliver to destruction a people who acts wickedly but still claims security as something it has by 'right' of its election by Yahweh.

In his commentary K. H. Graf says of the phrase 'a robbers' cave' (v. 11) that when a man is given over to such actions as have been described in the preceding verses and comes to the temple and imagines that he is free from all guilt and safe from all calamity, the temple is for him 'nothing other than the cave is for the robber, in which he seeks protection and refuge and from which he goes out to new crimes'.[45] But the evidence is in, and since Yahweh himself has 'seen it', no false witness or swearing (v. 9) on the part of the people will be able to gloss over the break in the relationship between him and his people.

Thus by uttering their lying words the people display an excessive confidence in a relationship to Yahweh which, it is felt, he will uphold almost unilaterally. Already the prophet's demand for repentance indicates what makes these words a lie: the relationship upon which they depend is not absolute but conditional. The verses which now follow provide the final statement in the case against the people: words of confidence, oaths in Yahweh's name, will be proven a lie by the destruction of the very thing which is the symbolic centre of this confidence, the temple, and the scattering of the people from their land.

The Temple Sermon concludes with the assertion that Yahweh has decreed the destruction of the temple (which would imply also

---

[45] Graf, *ad loc.*; characteristically, Volz remarks: 'But it is a monstrous insult to the moral God to suppose that his house can be a place of protection for an immoral people.'

the capture of the city) and the dispersion of the inhabitants of Judah. We notice that because of his own insights into the political and theological situation of his day, Jeremiah's own conception of 'Zion' does not carry with it the same sense of abiding security that it did for the prophet Isaiah. Instead of being the place which Yahweh will always protect, the place at which he appears to fight on behalf of his people, Zion is in Jeremiah primarily seen as the object of Yahweh's judgment. She is under attack by the enemies from the North (4.6, 31; 6.23), through whose agency Yahweh will actually destroy her (6.2; some dispute the text here).

It ought to be noted that even the excessive confidence attested by 7.4, 10 was not entirely effective in quieting the apprehensiveness of all the people. Both prophet (8.19) and people (14.19; cf. 9.18) could cry in despair that Yahweh was no longer in Zion protecting her. The same people who proclaimed 'This is the temple of Yahweh!' also remembered the century-old prophecy of Micah (3.12) concerning the destruction of Zion (cf. 26.18). Though the sense of security was firmly rooted in Israel's covenant traditions, the confidence which these produced was not absolute. For at least some people the awareness seems to have remained that the blessings of the covenants were conditional upon the people's and king's obedience to the covenant stipulations, and that destruction awaited the nation which sinned against Yahweh (8.14). Zion will be destroyed, and only after this act of punishment will she be vindicated by the defeat of Babylon (50.28; 51.10, 24, 35) and the ingathering of the dispersed into a reconstituted community of Yahweh (30.17; 31.6, 12; 50.5; cf. 3.14).

I Samuel 1.1–7.2 provides the background for the analogy which Jeremiah draws between the coming fate of Jerusalem and its temple and the past destruction of Shiloh. The Old Testament itself gives us no historical account of the destruction of that sanctuary, though it is often inferred from the account in I Samuel 4 of the great defeat suffered by Israel at the hands of the Philistines.[46] Psalm 78.56–66 also preserves the tradition that Yahweh

---

[46] The most recent examination of the archaeological evidence from Shiloh indicates a destruction of the city at the end of the eighth rather than the mid-eleventh century BC, raising the possibility that the city fell during Sargon's campaign against Samaria. Cf. Marie-Louise Buhl and Svend Holm-Nielsen, *Shiloh: The Danish Excavations at Tall Sailūn, Palestine, in 1926, 1929, 1932, and 1963* (Copenhagen: The National Museum of Denmark, 1969), pp. 61f. The

forsook his dwelling at Shiloh, delivered the ark into captivity, and gave his people to the sword because the people had forsaken him and refused to keep his 'testimonies'.[47]

Shiloh is not the only example available to us of Yahweh's turning against his sanctuaries (cf. Amos 3.14; 5.4f.) or cites (e.g., Samaria) because of the transgressions of the people, and so it might be asked why this particular location was chosen by the prophet to serve as an analogy to his contemporary act of judgment. The basis of the analogy would appear to be two-fold. First of all, Shiloh was the only locality that we know of outside Jerusalem where there was a temple of Yahweh (*bêth Yhwh*, I Sam. 1.7, 24; *hêkal Yhwh*, 1.9; 3.3). The sanctuary at Shiloh had housed the ark, the central symbol of the Sinai tradition. This ark was later taken by David to Jerusalem and subsequently housed in the temple there, which thus became Shiloh's successor as the main all-Israelite cult centre. Although the royal theology was apparently dominant in the Jerusalem cultus for centuries, since the time of Josiah there had been a renewed emphasis on the Sinai tradition there (cf. II Kings 23.24f., and the book of Deuteronomy). Furthermore, the family of priests located at Shiloh held their office by virtue of a decree that they should 'go in and out' before Yahweh 'forever' (*'ad 'ôlām*; I Sam. 2.30f.), but this agreement was revoked by Yahweh because of the wickedness of Eli's sons (cf. vv. 27–36). This state of affairs in which a group of sinful devotees is responsible for the revocation of Yahweh's promise reminds us of Jeremiah's polemic, and this similarity is further heightened by the fact that in both instances the people had attempted to exploit the relationship to their God to achieve security in a time of political distress (cf. I Sam. 4.3).

Secondly, the polemic of Jeremiah and the narratives about Shiloh mirror a similar set of conditions among the people. As we have noted, there is in each case a coupling of individual wickedness with external political crisis, but this in itself would not be

---

effectiveness of Jeremiah's analogy does not depend upon an actual destruction of the city by the Philistines, but upon the discrediting of the 'house' of Yahweh at Shiloh which resulted from the defeat of the Israelites and capture of the ark by the Philistines.

[47] The noun *'edûth* occurs frequently in connection with the covenant traditions. Sinai: Ex. 25.21f.; 32.15; Deut. 4.45; 6.20; Jer. 44.23; Ps. 99.7. David: II Kings 11.12; 23.3 (cf. I Kings 2.3); Ps. 132.12 (cf. 93.5).

Sufficient to distinguish these from the situation of Samaria in 722 (cf. II Kings 17.7–20). Like the Judeans at whom Jeremiah directed his polemic, the people of the Shiloh narratives suffered under a misconception of the basis of Yahweh's help and their security. The story clearly indicates that, when the battle began to go against them these men sent for the ark in an apparent belief that by bringing it to the field of battle they would guarantee Yahweh's intervention in their behalf: 'Why has Yahweh put us to rout today before the Philistines? Let us bring the ark of the covenant of Yahweh here from Shiloh, that he may come among us and save us from the power of our enemies' (I Sam. 4.3). It is against precisely such an easy, almost mechanical, attitude toward the security afforded by the people's covenant with Yahweh that Jeremiah argues in his Temple Sermon.

The analogy with Shiloh is thus the culmination of Jeremiah's line of reasoning in his denunciation of the people's over-confidence in Yahweh's protection. Yahweh has repudiated their conduct, and this will have the same historical result for temple, city, land, and people that his repudiation of a former generation's wickedness had for Shiloh.

The subject of this chapter has been the false conception of security which was held by many Judeans in Jeremiah's day. As described in Jeremiah 7.1–15, the temple is seen to be the symbolic focal point of this sense of security, and we have seen that the covenant traditions of the people provide the ultimate basis for their overconfidence. For Jeremiah such confidence was a 'lie' and its manifestations in such exclamations as 'This is the temple of Yahweh!' and 'We are delivered!' were 'lying words', trust in which would bring disaster. For while in fulfilment of his ancient promises Yahweh had established both the land and the kingdom 'forever', the covenants by which he did this were both conditional. The conditions of repentance announced by the prophet are related to both these covenants, and the loose attitude of the people toward these covenant regulations is part of what the prophet means when he charges that the people are trusting in a lie.

Although we cannot make a certain identification between the abuses which he cites and any particular cultic elaboration of *the* stipulations of the covenant, we can clearly see that Jeremiah considers the covenant relationship between Yahweh and his people to be broken. For the prophet knew that Yahweh makes certain demands upon his people, that by taking their election for granted (as a kind of guarantee of continuing security) the people had ceased to heed these demands, and that judgment would therefore be the inevitable result. To be Yahweh's people means to obey his commandments, but the people has not obeyed. Therefore, they are no longer his people. For the prophet it was as simple as that.

In fairness to the people, however, we must acknowledge that there were other equally intelligible patterns of reasoning at hand. The fact of the matter is that the ingrained covenant traditions and their attendant theology were essentially ambivalent in content. On the one hand they conveyed the surety that Yahweh had chosen to be this people's God and to act on their behalf, and, moreover, that he had done this despite what the people *were* (cf. Deut. 7.6–11). On the other hand, Yahweh demands obedience to the terms of the covenant, and will take into account what the people *are* in determining his future actions toward them (from the standpoint of Jeremiah's time he had already demonstrated this in the fall not only of Shiloh but also of Samaria; cf. II Kings 17.7–20).

We cannot, of course, assume that the people were aware of only the first of these points, or even that they were wholly indifferent to the second. It seems safe to assume, however, that there is something in human nature which led them to take the first more seriously and allow it to dominate their consciousness more fully. Their error was probably not so much that they denied that the covenant carried with it certain conditions, as that their view of salvation (based on their knowledge of election) as guaranteed did not permit them to take these conditions seriously enough. We are not here dealing so much with simple callousness or even naïveté as with a secure orthodoxy, fed by the 'forever' of the covenant traditions.

On the national scene this religious conviction contributed to a foreign policy which was ultimately disastrous. In the Temple Sermon we have revealed to us a frame of reference which helped make flying in the face of political realities (specifically, the rise to power of the Neo-Babylonian state) seem like a reasonable course of action. The prophet brands this confidence a 'lie'. It is so because, devoid of a living relationship to Yahweh, the people's

feeling of security is an illusion. It is powerless to deliver and
protect them in their time of national need. Such confidence is a
lie because it lacks power and is ineffective. Or perhaps one might
say that this lie is actually the possessor of a negative power.
Because of it the vital relationship between Yahweh and his people
is broken, and as a direct result of it the people will be destroyed:
'And now, because you have done all these things . . . I will cast
you away from me like I cast away all your brethren, all the seed of
Ephraim.'

II

CONFLICT WITH PROPHETIC OPPONENTS:
JEREMIAH 27–29

THERE are numerous oracles and narratives within the book of Jeremiah which show the prophet in conflict with opponents whose teaching he brands 'false'. It is to these passages that we now turn in our investigation of the use of the term *šeqer* in the message of Jeremiah. We will begin with an examination of chs. 27–29, a narrative the historical background of which is known to us and which provides us with information about several specific instances of conflict. In succeeding chapters we will deal with the complex of oracles directed against the prophetic opponents found in ch. 23, and finally with the scattered references to these prophets in Jeremiah's earlier oracles.

Before turning to the specific arguments about the nature of prophecy contained in chs. 27–29, there are two preliminary items which deserve comment. The first is a textual matter revolving around the fact that in these three chapters the LXX preserves a version of the narratives which is at points significantly shorter than that of the MT. The difference in length is in fact so striking that one recent commentator concludes, '. . . one is constrained to believe that LXX has the more original text, and that MT is a splendid illustration of the way in which the prose discourses of Jeremiah were verbally expanded in the course of transmission.'[1] Over a decade ago specific notice began to be taken of manuscripts from the caves of Qumran which shed light on the problems of the text and transmission of the book of Jeremiah.[2] More recently J. Gerald Janzen has been engaged in detailed studies of the text of Jeremiah which have led him to identify behind our MT and LXX two distinct 'text types', the Greek *'Vorlage'*

[1] J. Bright, *Jeremiah* (The Anchor Bible, Garden City: Doubleday, 1965), p. 202.

[2] Cf. F. M. Cross, *The Ancient Library of Qumran* (Garden City: Doubleday, 1958), p. 139.

deriving ultimately from an 'Egyptian Hebrew archetype.'[3] Though no effort will be made here to determine which of these texts should be given precedence, certain observations about the relationship between the two can be made.

The initial thing one notices about the relationship between the two texts is that LXX is almost always simply shorter than MT. Material found in MT but not LXX often runs into whole sentences (e.g., 27.7, 13f., 17f., 20; 29.14, 25) or even an entire paragraph (29.16–20). By contrast, there are only isolated words or phrases (e.g., 27.15, 16; 28.7, 10) which occur in LXX but not MT. The latter do not introduce new ideas, but are explicable in terms of their context. Thus several passages (27.9; 28.1; 29.1, 8) add the designation 'false' to MT's mention of Jeremiah's prophetic opponents, an addition easily understandable in a context which describes these opponents as men who spread 'lies' (cf. 27.10, 14, 16; 28.15; 29.9, 21, 23, 31).[4] Similarly, when 27.15 adds the word 'lie' to describe the nature of their prophecy and 27.18 finds LXX adding a comment by Yahweh that 'I did not send them,' we again seem to be dealing with a kind of narrative expansion which fits the picture of the prophets being developed in this context. Finally, the addition in 28.10 of the phrase 'in the eyes of all the people' can be understood as a narrative expansion heightening the tension of the scene depicting Hananiah's breaking of the yoke. Similarly, though the material peculiar to MT is sometimes lengthy, it is for the most part simply a narrative development of ideas or actions already present in both texts.[5]

[3] 'Double Readings in the Text of Jeremiah', *HTR* 60 (1967), pp. 433–47. This article is based on an unpublished dissertation, 'Studies in the Text of Jeremiah' (Harvard University, 1965).

[4] It has often been noted that Hebrew has no word for 'false prophet', and that the use of *pseudoprophētēs* constitutes an interpretation based on the context.

[5] In 27.5, for example, MT's 'the land, the cattle which are on the face of the earth' is a narrative expansion of a phrase common to MT and LXX ('I myself have made the earth') and adds nothing substantially new to the sense of the passage. Similarly in 28.3f. there are three lengthy phrases peculiar to the MT which do nothing more than add detail to Hananiah's assertion (common to both texts) that Yahweh will bring about a speedy end to the exile. Cf. also 27.13f., 17, 18–22 (expansions relating to the 'vessels' theme), 28.14, and 29.1, 6, as well as the summary statements of the charges against the opponents found in 28.16 and 29.21, 23. It is, of course, always possible that the absence of some of these phrases from the LXX may be explained as due to homoeoteleuton.

Some of the passages in question, however, do add elements which appear to be new to the narrative common to MT and LXX. The designation of Nebuchadnezzar as 'my (i.e., Yahweh's) servant' in 27.6 is an example of this, though we should remember that the idea here expressed is implicit in the command to the nations and to Judah to submit their necks to his yoke.[6] In 27.7 MT designates the length of service to Babylon as three generations, but although the idea is unique in this passage we may recall that in 29.10 LXX also contains the tradition that the exile will be of seventy years' duration. 29.14 speaks of an eventual ingathering of Yahweh's people from all directions, but we can note that the promise of a (perhaps more limited) return is a part of this context (v. 10). We arrive finally at 29.16–20, which scholars have traditionally considered to be a secondary intrusion. Rudolph (following Volz) argues that Jeremiah could not have sent a letter attacking the king by the hand of the king's own messengers (even if it were sealed?). More plausibly, he points out the fact that vv. 16ff. have little logical connection with v. 15.[7] When taken at their face value, these verses do constitute a rather startling digression from the topic at hand (i.e., life in the exile) and seem somewhat out of place in the overall structure of these chapters.

No real consensus has emerged as to which of the two textual traditions is to be considered the more 'original'.[8] For purposes of

---

[6] On this general problem see my 'King Nebuchadnezzar in the Jeremiah Tradition', *CBQ* 30 (1968), pp. 39–48.

[7] W. Rudolph, *Jeremia*, p. 186; cf. also J. P. Hyatt, *IB* V; E. A. Leslie, *Jeremiah*, p. 321; A. Weiser, *Das Buch des Propheten Jeremia, ad loc.*

[8] A final problem relating to the text is raised by the headings of 27.1 and 28.1, the former being wholly and the latter partially absent in LXX. 27.1 furnishes us with a date: 'In the beginning of the reign of Jehoiakim, son of Josiah, this word came to Jeremiah from Yahweh. . . .' The problem here is that this date is contradicted by the contents of the remainder of the chapter, which twice mention king Zedekiah (vv. 3, 12) and which obviously are set in a time after the exile of Jehoiachin (vv. 16f.). The MT of 28.1 adds: '. . . in that year, in the beginning of the reign . . .' (of Zedekiah), thus establishing a chronological connection between chs. 27 and 28. Rudolph agrees with LXX in omitting the heading of 27.1, arguing both from internal evidence and on the grounds that it jars with the new heading of v. 2 (*op. cit.,* 173f.). That the date supplied in 27.1 (MT) is in error seems a reasonable conclusion, especially in light of the fact to be demonstrated below that chs. 27–29 should be taken as a unit depicting Jeremiah's activity against his prophetic opponents in the context of the historical circumstances which prevailed in the period between the two deportations.

the following study the important conclusion resulting from the above investigation is that the narrative is in all its essentials the same, no matter which of the versions an investigator favours.[9]

The second of the preliminary matters which needs to be discussed is that of defining the nature of the cohesiveness of chs. 27–29. The fact is that in both style and content these chapters form a coherent, self-contained unit of narrative material, and our understanding of them will be aided if we can detect the nature and extent of that coherence. At the level of style, it has been recognized at least since the time of Giesebrecht that the chapters are characterized by several peculiarities which set them apart from the remainder of the book, notably the presence of both long and short spellings (sometimes in the same verse) of the proper names Jeremiah, Zedekiah, Jeconiah, and Hananiah; the prevalence of the 'n'-spelling of Nebuchadnezzar in contrast to the 'r'-spelling in the remainder of the book; and the use of formal titles (e.g., 'the prophet') with proper names.[10]

Moving beyond these stylistic features to the temporal sequence of the chapters, we may note that the narratives they contain seem to be arranged in chronological order. Even if this impression cannot be definitely proven, it is quite clear that at the very least these narratives refer to incidents which took place within the same precisely circumscribed period of time, namely, the reign of Zedekiah (597–586 BC) or, to put it another way, the period between the first and the second deportations of Judeans to Babylonia. Chapter 27 mentions both the fact that Zedekiah is king (vv. 3, 12) and that Jeconiah (Jehoiachin) in company with other Judeans and considerable booty has already been taken captive by Nebuchadnezzar and carried off to Babylon (vv. 16ff.). Further, the length of the exile is the main point being disputed in chs. 28 and 29 (cf. 28.1–4; 29.4ff., 24ff.). In favour of a chronological sequence we should remember the fact that ch. 27 has as its two main symbols the yoke which Jeremiah wears ('you must all submit your necks to the yoke of the king of Babylon') and the vessels of the temple which Nebuchadnezzar has carried off as booty ('they shall remain there indefinitely, until Yahweh is ready to restore them to this place'), and that it is precisely these two symbols which Hananiah takes up in his prophecy. For when

[9] The structural analysis which follows is based on MT.
[10] F. Giesebrecht, *Das Buch Jeremia*, pp. 146f.

Hananiah prophesies the early return of the vessels to Jerusalem
(28.3) and breaks the yoke-bars which Jeremiah has been wearing
on his neck, what can this be but a direct reply meant to contradict
the message of the prophet Jeremiah? Rudolph calls attention to
the fact that the 'and' of 29.1 serves to connect this chapter with
28, but admits that we cannot be absolutely certain that the connection between them is strictly chronological.[11] We may at least
observe that ch. 29 reports the extension of Jeremiah's message of
a long exile to the exiles themselves. At least one possible way of
explaining the necessity of this action would be to assume that the
increasing conviction among the Jerusalem officialdom that the
exile would shortly be over (Jeremiah was already fighting this
idea in the 'fourth year of Zedekiah', 28.1) had given rise to a false
hope among the exiles, which Jeremiah felt obliged to discourage.

Like others of the canonical prophets before him, Jeremiah was
very much aware of the political forces afoot in his day. The
thematic coherence of these three chapters is directly connected to
this awareness, for they are dominated by the prophet's conviction
that the authority of the newly-established Neo-Babylonian power
over the nations of Syria and Palestine was to be not simply a brief
interlude but a continuing political fact. It is, in other words, the
durability of Nebuchadnezzar's power which is really at stake in
the controversies of these chapters, Jeremiah remaining consistent
in his assertion:

Thus says Yahweh of hosts, God of Israel, 'I myself have made the
earth, the land, and the cattle which are on the face of the earth by my
great strength and my outstretched arm, and I will give it to whomever
is right in my eyes. And now I myself have given all these lands into
the hand of Nebuchadnezzar king of Babylon, my servant, and also the
living things of the field I gave to him to serve him. And all the nations
will serve him and his son and his son's son until the time of his land
also comes, and many nations and great kings will serve him. And it
will be that the nation and the kingdom which does not put its neck
in the yoke of the king of Babylon, I will visit that nation with sword
and famine and pestilence,' says Yahweh . . . (27.4–8).[12]

The political domination of Palestine by Nebuchadnezzar is thus
interpreted by the prophet as being due to Yahweh's explicit plan,

---

[11] *Op. cit.*, p. 182.
[12] Cf. also 27.11, 13, 22; 28.11, 14; 29.4–9, 28.

which no merely human decision to rise up in revolt can overcome.

In chs. 27–29 the matter of the duration of the exile of 597 tends
to be the specific point at which this question of the durability of
Babylonian power becomes an issue for argumentation (cf. 27.16,
21f.; 28.3f., 6; 29.28). It is this issue which comes to the fore in the
conflicts with prophetic opponents pictured there. We may note,
for instance, that the term *šeqer* occurs nine times in these chapters. In every instance but 29.21, 23 it is explicitly related to a false
prophecy which either counsels disobedience to Nebuchadnezzar
or insists upon the shortness of the exile. We may even assume
that the two exceptions mentioned are dealing implicitly with the
same theme, since the fact that these false prophets are punished
by Nebuchadnezzar would seem to indicate that the falsity of
which they were guilty had some sort of political overtones.[13]
This message that the exile will be short is false because it does not
correspond to Yahweh's plan for the permanence of Babylonian
power, and is in fact potentially dangerous, since the refusal to
accept the yoke of Babylonian authority can only result in denying
Judah and Jerusalem their one remaining chance for continued
independent existence (cf. 27.16ff.).

The impression of cohesiveness derived from our observations
about the style, temporal sequence, and theme of these chapters is
strengthened, finally, by a recognition of the structural pattern
according to which they are ordered. The chapters are dominated
by a particular kind of action, the conflict of Jeremiah with the
false prophets, which they elaborate upon in terms of the following general pattern:

A. Confronting the problem of false prophecy at home (27–28)
   1. *Message* of submission to Babylonian rule
      (addressed to the foreign messengers, to the king, and to
      the priests and people)
   2. *Negative response* to that message
      (Hananiah's symbolic action and prophecy)
   3. *Resolution*: curse on the one who rejects the message
      (death of Hananiah)

[13] So Rudolph, *op. cit.*, p. 185; Weiser, *op. cit.*, p. 256; Leslie, *op. cit.*, p. 213;
A. C. Welch, *Jeremiah: His Time and His Work* (Oxford: Blackwell, 1955), p.
166; F. Nötscher, *Das Buch Jeremias* (Bonn: Peter Hanstein Verlagbuchhand-
lung, 1934), p. 215; and Bright, *ad loc.*

B. Confronting the problem of false prophecy in Babylon (29)
  1. *Message* defining the length of the exile
  2. *Negative response* to that message by the prophets
      (vv. 15, 26–28, and implicitly vv. 21–23)
  3. *Resolution*: curse against the prophets
      (Ahab and Zedekiah, vv. 21–23; Shemaiah, vv. 30–32)

Both the ideas or theme common to chs. 27–29 and the outline or pattern in terms of which this theme is expressed oblige us in our exegesis to treat the passage as it now stands as a unit.[14]

The immediate historical background to this narrative unit is Jehoiakim's revolt against Babylon, which resulted in Nebuchadnezzar's first conquest of Jerusalem in 597. Although the cost of this revolt to Judah was great both in terms of damage done to her cities and of captives, booty, and territory lost,[15] yet within four years there are indications that the Jerusalem government was joining with neighbouring countries in plotting another attempt to throw off the yoke of the king of Babylon. Jeremiah 27–29 gives us our only information about this ferment, dating it in the year 594 (28.1). For some reason the plot was apparently never carried through, and the mission sent by Zedekiah to Babylon may have been for the purpose of reaffirming his loyalty to Nebuchadnezzar.[16]

There is clear evidence that national opinion was divided on the point of Judah's relationship to Babylon and that a division of party loyalties in the last decades before the exile was one of the stark political realities of the situation in which Jeremiah had to operate. We can trace the existence of these factions (which can be given names corresponding to their political orientations: pro-

---

[14] Whether this unity is original is a matter on which there may be differences of opinion. Rudolph, for example, asserts that it is not 'because' of the fact that these chapters belong to different sources: 28 and the genuine portions of 29 are 'B', but 27, which is in the first person and therefore cannot be 'B', is a 'series of speeches' based on genuine words of Jeremiah, i.e., 'A'. The peculiar style found here comes into existence with the combination of the three chapters, the purpose of which was to produce a '*Kampfschrift* against false prophets' who were too hastily awakening false political hopes regarding the exile (*op. cit.*, pp. 172f.). Note that the last statement implies that if the unity was not original it at least came about fairly early in the collection of the tradition.

[15] Bright, *A History of Israel*, p. 360.

[16] This is Bright's view, *ibid.*, p. 308. Cf. Jer. 29.3 and 51.59; the latter has Zedekiah himself making the trip to Babylon.

Egyptian and pro-Babylonian) through the reigns of the last five kings of Judah.

Josiah's policy of national expansion was anti-Assyrian, and, for that reason, also anti-Egyptian. As the result of pursuing this policy, Josiah was slain by Neco in 609, and was succeeded on the throne by his second son, Jehoahaz, who had the backing of the people of the land. The apparent anti-Egyptian orientation of this king and his backers is demonstrated by the fact that, after a reign of only three months, he was deposed by Pharaoh Neco, who replaced him with a man more sympathetic to the Egyptian cause, Jehoiakim. In a further move against his opposition, Neco levied a tax against the people of the land (II Kings 23.31–35).

This order of succession is itself revealing. Jehoahaz, who followed Josiah to the throne, became king at the age of twenty-three (II Kings 23.31), while Jehoiakim was twenty-five when Neco set him in his brother's place (v. 36). It is clear, then, that at Josiah's death the eldest son was by-passed in the selection of a successor, and the question is why this happened. One obvious answer would be that the choice was related to existing political sympathies. Those who supported Josiah's position (which at this point is probably better described as anti-Egyptian than pro-Babylonian) were still in power, and in Jehoahaz they may have recognized a man of their own political persuasion. When Neco asserted his power, however, a pro-Egyptian pretender, who also happened to be the real crown prince, was placed on the throne.[17]

The biographical narratives of the book of Jeremiah provide us with a picture of party factions during the reign of Zedekiah. In

[17] There is another detail which may be of some relevance here. Amon, Josiah's father, was the son of Meshhulemeth of Jotbah, a town which may be identical with the Galilean Jotapata of the Roman period (cf. L. H. Grollenberg, *Atlas of the Bible,* trans. and ed. by J. M. H. Reid and H. H. Rowley, New York: Nelson, 1957, p. 154). After a reign of two years, Amon was assassinated, and at this point the people of the land asserted their power, killing the conspirators and setting Josiah on the throne (II Kings 21.19–26). Now it is interesting to note that Josiah's mother, Jedidah, came from Bozkath, a town in central Judah (II Kings 22.1), and also that the two sons of Josiah who came closest to mirroring his political policy, Jehoahaz and Zedekiah, had a Judean mother (both were sons of Hamutal of Libnah; II Kings 23.31; 24.18). On the other hand, the pro-Egyptian Jehoiakim, like his grandfather, had a Northerner for a mother (Zebidah of Rumah in Galilee; II Kings 23.36). It may be that this geographical data relating to the queen mother is entirely coincidental, yet it may give us a hint that in some ways which are no longer very clear to us geographical location had something to do with political alignment.

fairness we must acknowledge that this king had many factors
working against him from the beginning of his reign: his youth
(he was twenty-one when he came to the throne, II Kings 24.18),
the operation of a strong pro-Egyptian faction among the
princes, the existence of the awesome power of Babylon, and the
complicating fact that the previous king, Jehoiachin, was still
alive and, though in captivity, considered by some to be the legitimate monarch.[18] The Jeremiah narratives portray him as a man
who was often in sympathy with the prophet, but who was powerless to act in the face of strong opposition among his own people
(Jer. 38.5; cf. vv. 24–26). The princes were thus in a position to
determine national policy, and that they were for the most part
pro-Egyptian in sentiment can be seen from some of their dealings
with the prophet. At one point, following a temporary lifting of
the siege, Jeremiah was apprehended as he was about to leave the
city and accused by the princes of deserting to the Babylonians
(37.11–15). They in fact regarded Jeremiah's whole message of
that period as treasonable, and sought his death on the grounds
that he was preaching that Jerusalem would fall to the Babylonian
army and was therefore weakening the defenders of the city and
not seeking the *šālôm* of the people (38.1–5). Although when all its
theological subtleties are taken into account the position of Jeremiah would probably have to be called something like 'pro-
Yahweh', on the strictly political level what we certainly see
mirrored here is the old division between pro-Egyptian and pro-
Babylonian loyalties.

All factors indicate, therefore, that the pro-Egyptian group was
in the position of dominance during the last two decades of the
nation's existence, but we do have some information regarding
supporters of the other side. What we know of this party centres
largely on the family of Shaphan, six members of which are
known to have been active during the reigns of the last five kings
of Judah. Shaphan ben Azaliah was Josiah's *sōphēr*. He served as
the middleman between the king and the high priest in the matters
of the repair of the temple and the transmission of the knowledge
of the newly-found book of the law. He was one of the four delegates whom Josiah sent to the prophetess Huldah, and we may

[18] Cf. W. F. Albright, 'The Seal of Eliakim and the Last Pre-Exilic History
of Judah', *JBL* 51 (1932), pp. 77–106, and 'King Jehoiachin in Exile', *BAR* I,
pp. 106–12.

assume that he was a strong supporter of the reform and of Josiah's policy in general (cf. II Kings 22.3–13). Shaphan had three sons about whom we have information: Ahikam (who was also one of the delegates to Huldah, and who later defended Jeremiah on the occasion of his Temple Sermon from those who wanted to put him to death; II Kings 22.12f.; Jer. 26.24), Elasah (one of Zedekiah's messengers to Nebuchadnezzar, who also carried Jeremiah's rather pro-Babylonian letter to the exiles; Jer. 29.3), and Gemariah (who was among those princes who were congregated in the temple, where they heard and were moved by the collection of oracles which Baruch had written on the scroll, and urged Jehoiakim not to burn the roll; Jer. 36.10–25). In addition two grandsons of Shaphan are mentioned: Micaiah ben Gemariah (who heard Baruch's first reading of the scroll and reported it to the other princes; Jer. 36.11–13) and Gedaliah ben Ahikam (whom seal evidence indicates was probably a 'chief minister . . . in Zedekiah's cabinet',[19] and who was appointed governor of Judah by the Babylonians after their destruction of Jerusalem in 586; II Kings 25.22; Jer. 40.5). The narrative also has it that Jeremiah was put under the latter's care when he opted against going to Babylon with the second group of exiles (Jer. 39.14; 40.1–6).

The evidence, therefore, tends to put Josiah, Jehoahaz, Jeremiah, and the family of Shaphan in a camp which opposed the pro-Egyptian policies of Jehoiakim and a large group of princes. In that sense at least, they may be called a 'pro-Babylonian' group. It would seem only reasonable to conclude that the relative sensitivity of persons to the theological burden of Jeremiah's message would in large part be affected by their own biases regarding the political situation.

Jeremiah's political sympathies are immediately apparent in ch. 27, the emphasis of which is upon the sharp contrast between Yahweh's power and will and the promise of the prophetic opponents of Jeremiah. Both what Yahweh has done and what he will do are stressed, the message being addressed to three audiences: the foreign messengers, the king of Judah, and the priests and people of Judah. Thus all of Judah's neighbours, as well as all the people of Judah herself, are (at least symbolically) warned in their turn against succumbing to the promises of the prophets who constituted a definite threat to the national well-being.

[19] Bright, *op. cit.*, p. 310.

The propagation of Jeremiah's message is set out in terms of the following scheme:

A. To the nations (vv. 3–11)
  1. What Yahweh has done
    (*a*) He is the creator (v. 5a)
    (*b*) He is the controller of creation (v. 5b)
    (*c*) He has given the creation over to Nebuchadnezzar (vv. 6f.)
  2. What Yahweh will do
  Nations who will not submit to Nebuchadnezzar's yoke will be punished by sword, famine, pestilence (v. 8)
  3. Exhortation
    (*a*) Do not listen to the prophets, diviners, dreamers, sorcerers, magicians who advise against serving Nebuchadnezzar
      (i) They are speaking *šeqer*
      (ii) Exile and destruction will be the result (*lema'an*)
    (*b*) He who submits to the yoke will be established

B. To Zedekiah (vv. 12–15)
  1. What Yahweh has done (omitted; already covered in vv. 5–7)
  2. What Yahweh will do (omitted; general statement given in v. 8)
  3. Exhortation
    (*a*) Put your neck in the yoke and live (vv. 12b, 13)
    (*b*) Do not listen to the prophets who advise against serving Nebuchadnezzar (vv. 14f.)
      (i)   They are prophesying *šeqer*
      (ii) Yahweh did not send them
      (iii) Exile and destruction will be the result (*lema'an*)

C. To the priests and all the people (vv. 16–22)
  1. (Omitted)
  2. (Omitted)
  3. Exhortation
    (*a*) Do not listen to the prophets who predict a speedy end to the exile (v. 16)
      (i) They are prophesying *šeqer*
    (*b*) Serve Nebuchadnezzar and live (v. 17)

4. A test for the prophets
   (*a*) The prophet as intercessor (v. 18)
   (*b*) The word to the temple furnishings (vv. 19–22)

Chapter 27 is thus divided into three sections, each of which contains a two-part exhortation: *do not* believe the prophetic *šeqer*, but *do* serve the king of Babylon. The two extra parts in section one are necessary to lay the groundwork for the exhortation (especially to foreigners, who would be unfamiliar with the prophetic view of Yahweh and his action), but need not be repeated.[20] The repetition of words and phrases makes it quite clear that these three sections are parallel:

(*a*) 'with sword and famine and pestilence'; verbatim, vv. 8, 13 (parts A, B)
(*b*) 'do not listen to (the words of) your prophets'; parallel, vv. 9, 14, 16 (A, B, C)
(*c*) 'for they are prophesying *šeqer* to you'; verbatim, vv. 10, 14, 16 (A, B, C)
(*d*) 'and live', etc.; vv. (11b), 12, (13a), 17a (A, B, C)

The message of Jeremiah is here set absolutely over against that of his prophetic opponents, although in contrast to ch. 28, the confrontation is not direct. It is simply assumed throughout that Jeremiah's message correctly mirrors the will of Yahweh. The ground-work for that message is laid with the assertion that it is Yahweh who created the earth and controls the course of events upon it. In light of the fact that in exercising this control he has given Syria and Palestine into the hand of the Babylonian king Nebuchadnezzar, any rebellion against the authority of that king is by definition an infraction of Yahweh's will.[21] The prophets who urge disobedience to Nebuchadnezzar show themselves to be utterly powerless. The inevitable result (*lᵉmaʿan*, vv.

---

[20] Weiser has a similar view of the omission of these preliminaries. He argues that when speaking to Israelites Jeremiah can presuppose the theological knowledge which will make the exhortation intelligible (*op. cit.*, p. 241).

[21] H.-J. Kraus has stressed the point that Jeremiah's conviction that Nebuchadnezzar was exercising his power in accordance with Yahweh's plan ought not be taken as simply an example of prophetic adeptness at political analysis. The Bible does not know our logical separation between politics and religion. Jeremiah's utterances rather proceed from the assumption of the reality of God's rule over all of history. *Prophetie in der Krisis* (Neukirchen: Neukirchener Verlag, 1964), pp. 74f.

10, 15) of listening to them will be death and destruction (vv. 8, 10, 13, 15, 17b), quite in contrast to the promise of life made by Yahweh to all who are obedient to his will (vv. 11, 12, 17a). The prophetic opponents' message of rebellion is a 'lie' just because it is powerless to prevent the catastrophe which awaits a disobedient people. Or perhaps it would be more accurate to say that their message does have a certain power, though it is decidedly a *negative* one, without the ability to save. For the message of rebellion, in so far as it obscures and glosses over the real situation, actually helps set the stage for the coming political catastrophe. It is Jeremiah's words of doom which ultimately bring salvation to the people, while the hopeful words of his opponents lead to their destruction.[22]

Jeremiah's opponents are often given the designation 'false' prophets, and it is important to get as clear a notion as possible of precisely wherein this falsity lies. We may begin by observing certain things which Jeremiah is *not* condemning in his opponents. In the first place, he is not condemning the prophets because of their association with other cultic functionaries (when addressing the foreign messengers, he can mention prophets in the same breath with diviners, soothsayers, etc.; v. 9) or because of their relationship to religious phenomena which transcend national boundaries (no distinction is made between the prophets of the nations and those addressed in Judah). There is no prejudicial language about any of the functionaries mentioned as such.[23] It is not the office as such but the content of the message delivered by the holder of that office which is repudiated. In the second place, it is not the notion of cultic prophecy which is here under attack. On the contrary, the call to intercession in v. 18 becomes a kind of test of true prophecy, and is in effect a call to perform a liturgical action.[24] Such intercession is not an unconditional proclamation

---

[22] Cf. *ibid.*, p. 77.

[23] It is interesting to note that in Jerusalem the prophet is the only functionary explicitly mentioned as a purveyor of false information.

[24] In his book *Liturgie und prophetisches Ich bei Jeremia* (Gütersloh: Verlagshaus Gerd Mohn, 1963) Henning Graf Reventlow puts forth the thesis that the prophetic office is characterized by a dual function which on the one hand requires Jeremiah to serve as Yahweh's messenger of judgment against a sinful people, while on the other enabling him to act as an intercessor, as the spokesman of the people before Yahweh. He therefore interprets 27.18 in this light, warning that it is wrong to see here a conflict between cultic and independent prophecy. At issue rather is the proper exercise of the prophetic

of peace, but it is an appropriate action precisely because, as Rudolph points out, the prophetic threat is never unconditional, for Yahweh is always free to change his plans for his people.[25] Finally, there is no indication of any alleged personal immorality of the opponents. The designation of these prophetic opponents as 'false' rests on nothing except the specific content of their message.

Throughout the book of Jeremiah one encounters a variety of suggestions as to what actually makes a prophet 'false'. While Yahweh appoints the true prophet (1.5), who then speaks in his 'name' (26.16), he does not 'send' the false prophet (14.14; 23.21-; 27.15; 28.15; 29.9). The erring prophets may be pictured as prophesying 'by Baal' (2.8; 23.13) or serving 'other gods' (2.26f.). They prophesy 'peace', or speak of Yahweh's unconditional protection, or of his inaction (6.13f.; 8.10f.; 14.13–16; 23.17; chs. 27–29). They are sometimes accused of being immoral (23.14f.; 29.21–23; on the interpretation of these passages see below), or speaking their messages on the basis of auto-inspiration (the visions of their own minds, 23.16; dreams, 23.25–32; traffic in oracles, 23.30f.). The problems involved with many of these criteria will be dealt with in the following pages. The account of Jeremiah's confrontation with Hananiah, to which we now turn, at least makes it obvious that the prophet had not worked out these criteria on a theoretical and systematic basis. He apparently had at his disposal no sure yardstick against which he could measure this opponent and refute his message on the spot.

Chapter 28 describes a specific confrontation of Jeremiah and one of these prophetic opponents, Hananiah. In outline the confrontation proceeds as follows:

---

functions. Intercession is a part of every prophet's function, and when properly exercised is not necessarily bound up with an easy proclamation of salvation (cf. pp. 188f.). It should be noticed that the intercessory function of the prophet is frequently mentioned in Jer.; cf. 7.16; 11.14; 14.11; 15.11; 17.16; 18.20; 21.2; 27.18; 37.3; 42.2, 4, 20; cf. also Kraus, *Prophetie* . . ., p. 80.

[25] *Op. cit.,* p. 162. G. Quell has also argued that (specifically with reference to Hananiah) a prophet's association with cultic prophecy is at most circumstantial evidence which has no necessary bearing on the validity of his particular message. *Wahre und Falsche Propheten* (Gütersloh: G. Bertelsman Verlag, 1952), pp. 51f.; also H. H. Rowley, 'The Unity of the Old Testament', *BJRL* 29 (1945–46), pp. 331f.

1. Hananiah appears and delivers his message: within two years the temple vessels and the exiles themselves will return from Babylon (vv. 1–4)[26]
2. The dialogue (vv. 5–11)
   (*a*) Jeremiah's rebuttal: 'Amen!', but tempered by a test for the legitimation of a prophet who brings a message of peace (vv. 5–9)
   (*b*) Hananiah's symbolic action (vv. 10–11a)
   (*c*) Jeremiah's response: withdrawal (v. 11b)
3. Jeremiah returns and (re-)delivers his message (vv. 12–16)
   (*a*) Breaking the yoke-bars has been pointless, since the threat which they symbolized still exists (vv. 12–14; 'for', v. 14)
   (*b*) The charge against Hananiah (v. 15)
      (i) Yahweh did not send him
      (ii) He causes the people to 'trust in *šeqer*'
   (*c*) The sentence (v. 16)
4. Narrative notation: the sentence carried out (v. 17)

Again, we shall do well to be aware of what judgments are not applicable to any argument that Hananiah is, in fact, a 'false' prophet. It cannot be charged, for example, that he speaks without obvious authority, for he comes forward to speak in the name of Yahweh (note the use of the messenger formula in vv. 2, 11) and succeeds in handing Jeremiah an apparent initial defeat. It is clear that Hananiah's 'falsity' is not immediately obvious to Jeremiah. Jeremiah is not here confronting a mere imposter. Hananiah is conscious of a prophetic call (cf. the messenger formula), and we have no reason to doubt his conviction that he speaks Yahweh's word. Here we have earnest men in opposition, prophecy against prophecy (insistence upon a lengthy duration of the exile against a definite prediction of an early return).[27] In contrast to 23.28

---

[26] Weiser comments that Hananiah's message is immediately understandable because of Jeremiah's previous warnings spoken in front of the salvation prophets, 27.(9), 14f., 16ff.; *op. cit.*, p. 245.

[27] So Rudolph, *op. cit.*, pp. 179; see also Weiser, *op. cit.*, p. 245; Leslie, *op. cit.*, p. 222; Quell, *op. cit.*, pp. 48f., 61. Beginning with the legal concept of 'false witness' (one who is not simply mistaken about the facts, but who consciously makes false statements), Quell protests that it is not quite fair to apply the term *šeqer* to Hananiah, from whose message indications of malicious falsity are absent. The most that can be said is that the fact of Babylon's

Hananiah is not attacked because of the form in which he received his revelation, and unlike the prophets Ahab and Zechariah (29.20–23) no mention is made of any personal immorality. Finally, even though Jeremiah himself mentions the fulfilment of prophecy as a check on the validity of Hananiah's message (v. 9) it is evident that the contest is not resolved on this issue. Jeremiah did not wait for two years to elapse before returning to confront his opponent, nor does he even mention the matter of nonfulfilment. He simply says, 'Listen now, Hananiah! Yahweh did not send you, and you are causing this people to trust in a lie. Therefore . . .' (v. 15).[28] To all outward appearances Hananiah was also a true Yahweh prophet. If he is to be shown to be otherwise, this

---

continued existence beyond the two-year limit and the fact of the second capture of Jerusalem meant that whoever trusted in the specific historical circumstances spoken of by this prophet trusted in a lie; pp. 16f. More will be said below about the problems of taking fulfilment as a criterion for judging between true and false prophecy. At any rate this means that Jeremiah's eventual use of the term *šeqer* with reference to Hananiah's message is as much an interpretation of the event as is the LXX's use of *pseudoprophētēs* throughout these chapters.

[28] Fulfilment of prophecy is one of the two criteria for judging a prophet proposed by Deuteronomy (18.21f.; the other is that the false prophet teaches rebellion against Yahweh, 13.2–6). Many have recognized the difficulties of appealing to this criterion: 1. A lapse of time, sometimes of considerable duration, is necessary before any prophecy can be recognized as either true or false. Micah's prediction of the destruction of the Jerusalem temple (3.12) waited for over a century for its verification. 2. We know of instances in which the great prophets themselves were wrong in their predictions. Isaiah was confident that the temple would never be destroyed (31.4f.; 33.17–22) but eventually it was, and the 'ass's burial' of Jehoiakim foreseen by Jeremiah (22.19) apparently never came to pass (cf. II Kings 24.6). 3. But as M. Buber suggests, even beyond these difficulties the 'very nature of prophecy . . . forbids' our using this criterion. Prophecy has the 'character of manifest or concealed alternative. . . . It is not whether salvation or disaster is prophesied, but whether the prophecy, whatever it is, agrees with the divine demand meant by a certain historical situation, that is important' (*The Prophetic Faith*, p. 178). In other words, prophetic utterances are often conditional by nature, uttered with the thought that the outcome will depend largely upon the people's response to the message (e.g., Amos 5.15). Cf. also Quell, *op. cit.*, pp. 55ff; G. A. Smith, *Jeremiah* (London: Hodder and Stoughton, 1923), p. 259; E. Jacob, 'Quelques remarques sur les faux prophetes', *ThZ* 13 (1957), pp. 479–81; E. Osswald, *Falsche Prophetie im Alten Testament* (Tübingen: J. C. B. Mohr, 1962), pp. 23–26. Kraus suggests that the death penalty levied against Hananiah was not based on a criterion of fulfilment, but on that of Deut. 13.2–6. He did not simply tell an untruth, but led the people away from Yahweh. *Prophetie . . .*, p. 102.

must be done from the point of view of the message with which he came before the people.[29]

The curious thing is that, when looked at outside its historical context, there is nothing particularly 'false' about Hananiah's message. In contradicting Jeremiah's veiled threat that far from a speedy return from exile there may well be a second plundering of Jerusalem (27.17ff.) with the assertion that the fortunes of Jerusalem are about to be restored (28.2–4, 10f.) Hananiah in fact stands firmly within the tradition of the prophet Isaiah, who was convinced that Zion would never fall.[30] Thus Kraus can say that in

[29] In a section of the monograph cited above, entitled 'Falsche Prophetie als innerjahwistisches Problem', Eva Osswald has done a striking job in pointing out the difficulties in distinguishing between true and false Yahweh prophets (pp. 12–26). Her method is to explore the criteria which the Old Testament itself uses to make such a distinction, and she discusses the following: 1. The form of the revelation. This criterion is not decisive because it does not apply to some of the most important of the prophetic opponents (e.g., Hananiah), as well as because some activity connected with the worship of Yahweh is legitimately mantic and dreams are sometimes positively valued (cf. I Sam. 28.6). 2. The consciousness of being sent. This criterion is ambiguous because it rests upon a personal experience the validity of which can only be asserted and not proven. The prophetic opponents also claim this certainty and preface their utterances with the messenger formula. 3. The trouble with the criterion of personal morality is that while some of the opponents (e.g., Hananiah) do not seem to have been guilty of immoral actions, the great prophets themselves sometimes acted rather immorally (e.g., Jeremiah's lie to the princes, 38.24ff.). 4. Objections to the criterion of fulfilment of prophecy have already been voiced in the preceding note. Micah 3.5–8 suggests another criterion, prophesying for pay. The objections to this will be dealt with later.

At its best a systematic use of such criteria results in inconsistencies and over-generalizations. At its worst it can lead to the acceptance of pious assumptions of doubtful value. E. F. Siegman's *The False Prophets of the Old Testament* (Washington, D.C.: The Catholic University of America, 1939) is an example of the latter. Siegman puts extreme emphasis upon accepting at face value the prophets' claims to supernatural inspiration, and makes use of the following criteria in his evaluation of the prophets: miracles, fulfilment of predictions, the sanctity of the prophets ('holiness of life,' 'singleness of purpose', 'absence of selfish motives'), and 'intrinsic criteria' ('Negatively, they are absence of error or contradiction of the legitimate religion of Israel; positively, they are the beauty and truth of this preaching, its lofty view of God, its insistence upon holiness of life, and its correct estimate of what favoured the progress of the theocratic state,' p. 83); cf. pp. 77–84. We are thus driven to a consideration of the message of these prophets to see if a more viable solution to the problem can be found there.

[30] For Isaiah of Jerusalem Zion is the place where Yahweh 'dwells' (8.18), and the tradition deriving from him bears witness to the significance of this place. The two most frequent things which the Isaiah tradition says about Zion are that it successfully withstands all attacks (1.7f., 24–28; 14.32; 29.8;

Hananiah we meet 'the prophetic exponent of an Israelite salvation theology founded in election and covenant'.[31]

This fact in itself should make us wary of attributing too much significance to the criterion which Jeremiah himself apparently sets up in 28.8f., namely that a prophecy of peace must be validated by its fulfilment, while a prophecy of doom (because of the precedent of previous prophets) need not be. Rudolph has pointed out that if we interpret this statement to mean that no great prophet may utter any words of hope, Jeremiah himself would have to be judged a false prophet. He therefore sees the contrast as one between the great prophets, whose message has predominantly been one of doom, and the 'nothing-but-salvation-prophets', who have been so often wrong that one is forced to adopt the criterion of Deut. 18.21f. regarding them.[32] In an early article dealing with this problem of false prophecy G. von Rad argued for the existence in Israel of a succession of institutional prophets whose task was not (as it was in the case of Amos) to stir up the people, but rather to function in the office of intercessor. The fact that a prophet could function as an intercessor was read back by 'E' into the time of Abraham (Gen. 20.7), appears in connection with the Isaiah legends of II Kings (19.1ff.), and may be found also in Jeremiah (27.18; 37.3; 42.2, etc.). Such intercession for the peace of 'this place' is naturally connected with the immunity of the Jerusalem temple (cf. Jer. 14.13; Micah 3.11). When we remember that over a period of several hundred years the hope for peace had largely been fulfilled (Jerusalem was never captured by a non-Israelite aggressor from the time of David until the last days of the prophet Jeremiah) and also that the notion of security which it involves stands in the context of a great covenant theology which pervades much of the Old Testament literature, it should be evident that the mere fact that a prophetic message was one of peace would not in itself be enough to brand it as being

---

30.19; 31.4f.; 33.1–24; 34.8; 37.22, 32) and is the centre around which the life of the people and the nations will be reconstituted (2.2–4; 4.2–6; 11.1–12.6; 16.1–5; 24.21–23; 35.8–10).

[31] *Op. cit.*, p. 91.

[32] *Op. cit.*, p. 180. Rudolph thinks that what Jeremiah is really saying is: I have the great prophets on my side and no one doubts their verity (cf. 26.17ff.), but the verity of the prophets of salvation is in doubt.

false.[33] On the basis of visions, laments, and other passages found in the book of Jeremiah, Henning Graf Reventlow has recently argued persuasively that intercession on behalf of the people forms at least one part of the prophet's function.[34]

This means that the problem to be faced here is not one involving the prophetic message abstracted from its historical context. Von Rad recognized this when he interpreted the confrontation between Jeremiah and Hananiah as raising the question of the correspondence between prophecy and history. Since for Israel history was the place 'in which Yahweh's rule was recognizable', this becomes the crucial issue in the problem of false prophecy.[35] It is the historical context which makes an otherwise unobjectionable message 'false'. Hananiah had been guilty of a misreading of Israel's election faith. It is certainly true that Yahweh has chosen this people and wills their salvation (cf. Deut. 7.7ff.; 12.9ff.; 20.4), but Hananiah had apparently forgotten that the covenant also carries with it definite obligations which the people must be careful to fulfil. He had apparently not interpreted the political events of his day as being a punishment levelled by Yahweh against a sinful people. He had applied an *old* message in a *new* situation, and had thus demonstrated '. . . *the inability to orient himself in the new historical situation,* viz. to perceive the will of God for a specific situation and at a specific place'.[36] Hananiah spoke from within Judah's living cultic tradition, but in this instance tradition, with its eyes focused on the past, became an obstacle which hindered him in his task of attempting to discern Yahweh's will in the present moment.[37]

---

[33] 'Die falschen Propheten', *ZAW* 51 (1933), pp. 109–120. Along these same lines cf. J. Lindblom, *Prophecy in Ancient Israel,* p. 215.

[34] *Op. cit.*; cf. p. 36, n. 24 above. By comparing these passages with the ritual pattern of lamentation followed by an oracle of salvation known from other portions of the Old Testament and by taking the cultic *Sitz im Leben* very seriously, he is able to point to a number of passages which reflect Jeremiah's performing of this function.

[35] *Op. cit.,* p. 119.

[36] Osswald, *op. cit.,* p. 21; cf. Leslie, *op. cit.,* pp. 222f.

[37] Cf. T. C. Vriezen, *An Outline of Old Testament Theology,* trans. S. Neuijen (Oxford: Blackwell, 1958), p. 71. E. Jacob has suggested several such obstacles which could stand in a prophet's path: royal control (cf. I Kings 22), tradition, the crowd, the desire to be successful. The second of these seems definitely to apply to Hananiah (*op. cit.,* pp. 483–86). The aspect of pressure from the crowd probably ought not be completely overlooked, since it is clear that the people sometimes sought to exercise control over a prophet either by forbidding him

Perhaps it would be best to say that in the confrontation of Hananiah with Jeremiah we witness the clash of two widely-differing interpretations of the nature of Yahweh's action within Judah's present history. The message of the former has its roots sunk deep into the promises of security, of Yahweh's positive action on behalf of his people, embodied in the religious forms of the past (the covenant traditions). From this point of view it must have been self-evident that a nation like Babylon, which infringes Yahweh's eternal order, must fall. As Quell has suggested, for him the first exile was the low point, and the fact that anything remained of Judah at all must have seemed a divine miracle, the point of contact for a confidence that God was still with his people (cf. Jeremiah's attitude in 29.11). The events of 597 must have given occasion for many to feel that Yahweh had forsaken his land. 'Hananiah tells them what faith in God is, just as Isaiah had told Ahaz.'[38] In short, 'Hananiah had acted impulsively, perhaps in wrath, but in a strong consciousness of the divine commission.'[39]

But it was at just this point that Hananiah ceased to act like one of the classical prophets. For while it was true that one of the constant factors in the message of all these prophets was the theology of the election tradition in which they stood, their preaching was also characterized by a second, extremely important factor: a new word of Yahweh addressed to the current life-situation of the people. As von Rad has described it, these prophets had 'a keen and unprecedented awareness of the great historical movements and changes of their own day and generation', and their whole preaching was 'quite new' in its ability to adjust and adapt to the events of that history. 'This correlation between the prophets and world-history is the real key to understanding them correctly, for they placed the new historical acts of God which they saw around them in exactly the same category as the old basic acts of the canonical history. . . .' In fact they came to realize that in his new historical actions Yahweh was superseding the old and 'bringing about a new era for his people'.[40] To put the matter in Lindblom's terms, the 'new discovery' of the prophets

---

to speak or expecting that his message reflect a certain content which would be pleasing to them; cf. Isa. 30.8–14; Jer. 11.21; 26.7–11; 38.4; ch. 42.

[38] Quell, *op. cit.*, p. 59; cf. pp. 55ff.

[39] *Ibid.*, p. 61.

[40] *Theology* II, pp. 112f.; cf. also II, p. 130.

was that this chosen people 'had fallen away from Yahweh . . . had been rejected as a nation and would be punished.'[41]

Hananiah belonged to that group of Judeans which had come to view the old forms of the people's relationship to Yahweh as being permanently valid. In practice this meant that the God of Judah was thought to be unconditionally bound to protect his people, to act positively on their behalf, no matter what their attitude towards his commandments might be (recall 7.1–15). This way of thinking in effect closed their eyes to the facts of the historical situation in which they stood. Nebuchadnezzar's authority was by this time firmly established, and revolt against it could have no other result than political disaster. Only a stereotyped conception of Yahweh's relationship to them could blind religious people to this fact.

Jeremiah, on the other hand, was extremely sensitive to the people's unwillingness, even inability, to remain faithful to the demands imposed upon them in the old covenant relationship (cf. 2.20–22; 13.20–27). He was thus able to interpret the present destructive course of events as being nothing other than the negative activity of a God who now found it necessary to punish his sinful people. This does not mean that Jeremiah's assessment of the stability of Neo-Babylonian power would necessarily have to have been proven correct. We can easily imagine any number of contingencies which would have drastically altered the balance of power in Syria-Palestine. Even the fact that he did eventually prove to have been accurate in his analysis of the situation is not entirely relevant, for we have seen that there are grave difficulties associated with any appeal to the criterion of fulfilment. What is important is that Jeremiah's freedom to transcend the old traditions and offer a new interpretation of the people's present situation is based ultimately in his recognition of Yahweh's freedom to change the forms through which he will relate himself to his people. Thus in the context of Jerusalem between the two deportations the message of Hananiah proved to be false because, as Quell puts it, it embodied too naïve and simple a view of faith in the saving power of God.[42]

Jeremiah was at first forced to accept Hananiah's message, and despite some misgivings he 'went his way' (28.11). Yet apparently

14 *Op. cit.,* pp. 311f.
42 *Op. cit.,* p. 65.

within a short time he returned to confront his opponent a second time. He begins by reiterating his original message: in place of the broken yoke of wood will be put a yoke of iron, for the nations will indeed be forced to serve the king of Babylon. This re-affirmation of his message is followed by a charge directed at the opponent: 'Listen now, Hananiah! Yahweh did not send you, and you are causing this people to trust in a lie' (v. 15). In light of the above discussion the first element of this charge might be para-phrased as follows: 'Yahweh did not send you in *this* situation with *this* particular message.' And because of this fact the breaking of the yoke bars has been pointless. It was a dramatic and doubt-less moving action, but it was powerless to alter the course of events willed by Yahweh. Hananiah had caused the people to 'trust in a lie' precisely because his message had only obscured, but had not been effective in eliminating, the danger which was threatening the land of Judah in his day.

We come finally to ch. 29, which documents Jeremiah's hand-ling of the problem of false prophecy among the exiles. The contents of this chapter may be outlined as follows:

A. The letter to the exiles (vv. 1–23)
  1. Description of the sending of the letter (vv. 1–4)
  2. The message of the letter (vv. 5–23)
     (*a*) Advice on the problem of the duration of the exile
        (i) Lead a normal and productive life in Babylon (vv. 5f.)
        (ii) Seek the good for your captors (v. 7)
        (iii) Do not heed the *šeqer* prophets and diviners (whom, we must infer, are predicting an early return from exile, vv. 8f.)
        (iv) Restoration will come, but only after seventy years (vv. 10–14)
     (*b*) The problem of prophecy in the exile
        (i) Provocation: the people have claimed that they have prophets in exile (v. 15) (intrusion: against the king in Jerusalem, vv. 16–20)
        (ii) Verdict against the *šeqer* prophets, Zedekiah and Ahab (vv. 21f.)
        (iii) Charge against Zedekiah and Ahab: immorality and *šeqer* (v. 23)

B. The controversy over Jeremiah's interpretation of the exile: the interrelationship of the opponents at home and in the exile (vv. 24–32)

    1. The report of Shemaiah's attempt to repress Jeremiah (vv. 24–28)

    2. The report of how Jeremiah became aware of this attempt (v. 29)

    3. Jeremiah's rebuttal of Shemaiah's *šeqer:* his family will not survive to see the restoration (vv. 30–32)

One has little difficulty noting the similarity of the three episodes in which Jeremiah is shown dealing with specific false prophets. First, we observe that in two of the three cases these prophets oppose his interpretation of the exile by claiming that it will be of only short duration (Hananiah, 28.2–4, 11; Shemaiah, 29.28). The case of Ahab and Zedekiah is less clear, for the content of their message is not specifically mentioned. That their activity had political overtones, however, seems to be implied, since it would otherwise be difficult to account for their punishment by the hand of Nebuchadnezzar's agents. It is not easy to understand why the Babylonian officials would involve themselves directly with these men if the basic issue at stake were simply a matter of personal immorality among the captives (v. 23: '. . . they commit adultery with the wives of their companions . . .'), but if they too were preaching an early return from exile, we might well imagine that this message would be interpreted by the Babylonians as incitement to rebellion. Such actions would indeed justify their direct intervention. Second, in all three cases Jeremiah uses the term *šeqer* to characterize the message of his opponents (Hananiah, 28.15; Ahab and Zedekiah, 29.23; Shemaiah, 29.31).[43] Finally, in the course of his polemic Jeremiah condemns each of his opponents to death (28.16f.; 29.21f., 32). One ought also to note that in the course of the 'letter' in which Jeremiah describes to the captives the duration of the exile he mentions in a general way the fact that prophets and diviners have contradicted his view on this

[43] 20.6 is another instance in which Jeremiah uses the term *šeqer* to describe an opponent (Passhur, a temple official who abused him after he predicted the coming destruction of the city). The branding of opposing views with this term is remarkably infrequent outside Jeremiah (cf. Isa. 9.14; Ezek. 13.22; Zech. 13.3), a fact which serves to stress the importance of that term for understanding the peculiarities of the theology of the Jeremiah tradition.

matter. Here again we meet the familiar charge that this opposing opinion is *šeqer*, and that Yahweh did not 'send' them (29.9). We have already seen that the first element of this charge is specifically repeated with regard to each of the opponents named, and the same is true of the second element: Yahweh 'sent' neither Hananiah (28.15) nor Shemaiah (29.31), and he did not 'command' Ahab and Zedekiah to deliver their message to the people.

Chapter 29 does introduce one new element into the charges made against the prophetic opponents, namely the allegation of personal immorality levelled against Ahab and Zedekiah (v. 23). Rudolph feels that for Jeremiah this 'moral failing' of the two prophets was 'irrefutable proof' that their religious message is unreliable.[44] Weiser elaborates on this point, citing other occurrences of the phrase 'do foolishness in Israel'[45] and noting that in the law adultery is a sin punishable by death (Deut. 22.22). Here for Jeremiah is 'proof' that these men cannot be true prophets of Yahweh. 'With the moral earnestness of conduct stands and falls not only the trustworthiness of the proclamation, but also the genuineness of the faith itself. The two are not to be separated; God's Word is only perceptible in moral obedience.'[46] These observations may well be correct, and we will have to return again to the problem of prophetic immorality in the following investigation of ch. 23. For the present, however, it is sufficient to refer to what has already been said about the political implications of the punishment of Ahab and Zedekiah and to recall that the main issue in the chapters under discussion is the content of the message of the prophetic opponents. Even in the case of Ahab and Zedekiah it is this message and not the personal conduct of the prophets (which in the cases of Hananiah and Shemaiah was apparently above reproach) which Jeremiah brands as *šeqer* and against which he wages bitter battle (v. 23b).

As in the case of Hananiah (cf. 28.15), it is said of Shemaiah that he caused the people to 'trust in a lie' (29.31). It is clear that the

---

44 *Op. cit.*, p. 169.

45 The passages cited are Gen. 34.7 (in the story concerning Shechem's rape of Dinah), Judg. 20.7, 10 (the Benjaminites' abuse of the Levite's concubine), II Sam. 13.20 (Amnon's rape of his sister Tamar), and Deut. 22.21 (the law stipulating that a bride found not to be a virgin is to be stoned). It is to be noted that in each case the action is considered to be an offence of the utmost seriousness, and death eventually overtakes its perpetrator.

46 *Op. cit.,* p. 256.

primary referent of this phrase is these prophets' insistence that
the time of restoration of exiles and booty to Judah is near at hand.
We will not be amiss, however, in calling attention to similar
expressions in ch. 7, where the people are chided for trusting in
'lying words' (vv. 4, 8) or in 'the house which is called by my
name' (v. 14). The topic under discussion there is, of course, a
false trust which was grounded in the covenant traditions and
found its symbolic focal point in the temple. We have repeatedly
seen how the message of peace proclaimed by the prophetic
opponents of chs. 27–29 bears an intimate relation to this confidence in the assured security of Jerusalem and her temple
(Jerusalem will be restored and not further ravaged, the temple
implements will be restored, etc.). It is thus clear that there is an
intimate relationship between Jeremiah's polemic against the falsehood of a general misconception of the nature of the people's
security and that of the prophetic opponents. For the message of
the latter takes up the themes of the former, and it is in the message
of these opponents that their falsity lies. Theirs is a message which
is ineffective because it is simply powerless to change a situation
which Yahweh wills.[47] Theirs is a message which, however true it
may be in abstract principle, is in its historical context potentially
very dangerous, for it obscures the real political situation (as well
as possible avenues for making theological sense of this situation)
and builds false hopes which eventually lead to the downfall of
Judah.

[47] In this respect we may notice the interesting parallels between the conflict of Jeremiah with Hananiah and that of Micaiah with the court prophet
Zedekiah (I Kings 22): both involve a symbolic action and the physical abuse
of one prophet by the other (I Kings 22.24), and in both the criterion of
fulfilment is mentioned (I Kings 22.25, 28). But it is the outcome of the
opponent's message which is of most interest. Micaiah speaks of a *šeqer*-spirit
which has enticed the prophets to encourage the king to embark upon a course
of action which cannot be brought to a successful conclusion because Yahweh
is against it. In direct analogy with the people who listen to Hananiah's
message of encouragement the king's acceptance of this *šeqer* places him in a
situation where he will be ineffective in his attempt to wage a successful
battle. And in both cases the *šeqer* has a certain negative power, for in effect
it brings about the king's defeat.

III

ORACLES AGAINST THE PROPHETIC OPPONENTS:

JEREMIAH 23.9–40

In his description of the oracular materials incorporated within the book of Jeremiah, W. Rudolph points to four instances in which longer complexes with special superscriptions have been taken up as units: 14.1–15.3 ('concerning the drought'); 21.11–23.8 ('to the house of the king of Judah'), 23.9–40 ('to the prophets'); and 46.1–49.33 ('concerning the nations').[1] The third of these groups has been described as '. . . mostly small fragments, which have the prophets as their subject. As usual in such cases, a few oracles are clearly defined near the beginning of the little collection, e.g., 9–11, 13–15, 21–22, 23–24, 25–29 (much modified), 33–40 (also much worked over).[2] Oesterley and Robinson thus point to the thematic unity of this complex when they note that the prophets are here the main topic of discussion. To be more specific, Jeremiah 23.9–40 constitutes an attack on the false message of Jeremiah's prophetic opponents. To this attack we now turn our attention.

Jeremiah's Lamentation over the Land (9–12)

9 To the prophets:[3]
My heart is broken within me,
    all my bones tremble:
I am like a drunken man,
    and like a strong man whom wine overcomes;

[1] *Op. cit.,* p. xv.
[2] W. O. E. Oesterley and T. H. Robinson, *An Introduction to the Books of the Old Testament* (London: SPCK, 1934, reprinted New York: Meridian, 1958), pp. 296f.
[3] The differences between LXX and MT are not nearly so extensive here as was the case in chs. 27–29; substantive differences are minimal.

```
              because of Yahweh
              and because of his holy words.
   10  For the land is full of adulterers;
           for because of the curse the land mourns,
              the pastures of the wilderness are withered;
           their course is evil,
              and their strength is not right.
   11  For both prophet and priest are profaned,
           even in my house I have encountered their evil,
                                             says Yahweh.
   12  Therefore their way will be for them like slippery places
                                             in the darkness;
           they will be cast down,
              and they will fall in it;
           for I am bringing evil against them,
              the year of their visitation,
                                             says Yahweh.
```

The language with which this section begins has its home in the sphere of the lamentation, and indicates how personally devastating was the prophet's perception of the present condition of his people. Thus Jeremiah's reference to his broken heart is reminiscent of the psalmist's cry, 'An insult has broken my heart . . .' (Ps. 69.21), and the following reference to 'trembling' bones and drunkenness adds to this effect, since the characteristic action of a drunkard is to stagger about in a confused, chaotic fashion. The total picture conveyed is one of a prophet who is extremely agitated and unsettled by what he sees in the land.

In the first verse we learn that the estrangement between Yahweh and the land is the cause of Jeremiah's lamentation. In v. 10 this estrangement is described in terms of a pattern of conduct (a*a*) which has led to the drought that is weakening the land (a*b*) and has caused the distress of its animal population (b). It is the term 'adultery' which is chosen to describe the conduct of the people. On the one hand what is being discussed here is a social and moral offence, but it should not be forgotten that the term is often used by Hosea and Jeremiah in connection with Baal worship in general or cultic prostitution in particular.[4] The thing to be noticed is that in both cases the 'adultery' constitutes an infraction of the covenant stipulations, and thus furthers the estrangement of

---

[4] Cf. Jer. 3.8f.; 13.27; Hos. 2.4; 4.13f. In Jer. 3.1–5 this concept is also present, though the term *n'ph* does not appear. Cf. Kraus, *Prophetie . . .*, pp. 29f.

the people from their God. As to the term 'pasture' (or 'habitation'), we rarely find it in a straightforward narrative context. Rather, the reference is typically to the land as the object of Yahweh's action, whether that action be destructive[5] or constructive[6] in nature. In the case of the former the lament context again predominates.

Verse 11 is an indictment of prophet and priest. The charge is that these officials are 'profaned', that is, that they have been removed from their close relationship to the holy God. It is true that such profanation can be something which is forced upon one, as Zion would be profaned should a foreign power capture her (Micah 4.11). Yet most often the Old Testament pictures profanation as the result of one's own actions, the result of one's transgression of the covenant commandments.[7] The indictment is followed in v. 12 by a proclamation of judgment, expressed in stereotyped terms. The concrete form of the punishment is not yet clear, although it is clear that the punishment is viewed as coming from Yahweh himself.[8] In language closely paralleling that of the present passage the suppliant of Psalm 35 calls upon Yahweh to take vengeance against his enemies:

> Let their path be dark and slippery places,
>   and the angel of Yahweh pursuing them! (v. 6)

And as for the 'darkness' (*ªphēlā*) in which the people will tread their slippery path, in no case does this term refer merely to the darkness of night which naturally follows the light of day. It is rather the darkness which characterizes the life of the unrighteous (Isa. 8.22),

---

[5] Eg., Isa. 27.10; Ps. 79.7 (communal lament); Amos 1.2; Lam. 2.2; Jer. 9.9; 10.25.

[6] With reference to the restoration of Israel in or to her land, cf. Joel 2.22; Ps. 65.13; Isa. 33.20; 35.7; 65.10; Jer. 31.23; 33.12; 50.19; Ezek. 34.14.

[7] Cf. Isa. 24.5, where the land is profaned because of the transgressions of its inhabitants. Again, the offence can be either social or religious in nature. Jer. 3.1 pictures an actual case of harlotry, but vv. 2, 9 show that the same result stems from apostasy (here described as harlotry). Acquittal of murderers brings a bloodguilt which profanes the land (Num. 35.33), but the same holds for the bloodguilt coming through the practice of child sacrifice (Ps. 106.38).

[8] The word is used with designations of time to suggest an unspecific future date of punishment: 'day of punishment' (Isa. 10.3; Hos. 9.7; Micah 7.4), 'year of punishment' (Jer. 11.23), 'time of punishment' (Jer. 8.12; 46.21). In all instances in which the noun *pequddah* means 'visitation' or 'punishment' rather than simply 'commission' or 'office', Yahweh is designated as the agent responsible for its coming.

and especially that which is sent by Yahweh against the wicked. It is the darkness of an Egyptian plague (Ex. 10.22), a darkness at noonday which is part of the curse levelled against those who break the covenant stipulations (Deut. 28.29), or the darkness of the approaching terrible 'day of Yahweh' (Joel 2.2; Zeph. 1.15). It is the task of the following section to make the nature of this punishment more specific.

The Coming Destruction (13–15)

13 And among the prophets of Samaria I saw an offensive thing:
    they prophesied according to Baal,
    and led my people Israel astray.
14 Also among the prophets of Jerusalem I have seen a horrible thing:
    committing adultery
       and walking in the lie;
    and they strengthened the hands of evildoers,
       in order that no one (need) turn from his evil.
They have all become to me like Sodom,
    and her inhabitants like Gomorrah.
15 Therefore thus says Yahweh of hosts against the prophets:
    Behold I am feeding them on wormwood,
       and giving them poison water to drink;
for from the Jerusalem prophets alienation has gone out
                 to the whole land.

The 'prophets' mentioned in the heading of v. 9 as the targets of the utterance which follows are not explicitly identified, though the implication is clear that they are those of Judah (remember the reference to the actions of prophet and priest in 'my house', v. 11). The *waw* at the beginning of v. 13 indicates a simple connection with the preceding section, and thus the main object of attention of v. 13–15 is also the Jerusalem prophets.

The *waw* at the beginning of v. 14 has often been taken as introducing an antithesis. The Revised Standard Version translates:

    In the prophets of Samaria I saw . . .
    But in the prophets of Jerusalem I have seen . . .

Giesebrecht, Rudolph, Weiser, and Bright arrive at similar results. The implication of such a translation is that Samaritan idolatry was bad enough, but Judean prophecy was even worse, due to the

added element of moral degradation.[9] Leslie translates the *waw* as
'Aye . . .', but his interpretation is still moral. Jeremiah is con-
trasting the activities of contemporary prophets in Samaria with
those of Jerusalem: 'But even in Jerusalem, where the moral and
spiritual voices of the prophets Amos, Isaiah, and Micah had
already been heard, conditions were little better. Indeed, the
situation was utterly disgusting.'[10]

But there is an alternative to this moralistic interpretation. The
main point of vv. 13–15 is not morality, but the *nature of the judgment* against the prophets and the whole land. This section therefore forms a continuation of the preceding one, which ends with a
threat of punishment couched in stereotyped language. The nature
of the judgment is left unclear, and it is the function of vv. 13–15
to give specific content to this proclamation.

The prophets of Samaria being referred to here are those of the
period before 722 BC. I Kings 22 gives us one view of them and
their activity. It is Jeremiah's conviction that they led their people
astray, and although the result of this wandering off Yahweh's
paths is not explicitly mentioned, everyone is aware of it: namely,
the destruction of the Northern Kingdom by Shalmanaser V in
722 (recall how the prophet employed a similar historical argument in 7.1–15 by mentioning the fate of Shiloh).[11]

Already before 722 the worsening situation in Samaria was
interpreted by Hosea as being due to the fact that Ephraim
'incurred guilt through Baal and died' (13.1), a passage which
H.-W. Wolff places within the context of Tiglath-peleser's conquest of Galilee and Transjordan in 733.[12] Worshipping Baal is
one of the specific cultic indictments levelled against Israel by the
Deuteronomic historian in his explanation of the fall of Samaria
(II Kings 17.16). Although it is true that II Kings 17.7–18 may
well be post-exilic in date (the inclusion of Judah in the fate of
Israel, v. 13, seems to indicate this), J. Gray has pointed out that
the 'D' school was in existence before the exile and there is no

[9] Rudolph gives vv. 13–15 the title 'the immorality of the prophets',
op. cit., p. 151.
[10] *Op. cit.,* p. 225.
[11] There has been some debate on the matter of the exact date of Samaria's
fall and the identity of her captor (Sargon II also claims that victory). Cf.
E. R. Thiele, *The Mysterious Numbers of the Hebrew Kings* (2nd ed. rev.; Grand
Rapids: Eerdmans, 1965), pp. 141–54.
[12] *Dodekapropheton 1: Hosea,* pp. 291f.; notice that the same phrase, 'by
Baal', occurs in both Hos. 13.1 and Jer. 23.13.

reason even to suppose that it was newly born in 622.[13] Likewise
M. Noth, who argues that the Deuteronomic historian was an
author who wrote his history in the mid-sixth century, recognizes
that his theological interpretation was influenced by the ideas of
the Deuteronomic law stemming from the time of Josiah.[14] We
are therefore safe in assuming that this interpretation of the fall of
Samaria was known to at least some Judeans in Jeremiah's time.

In v. 14 we encounter Jeremiah's charge against the Jerusalem
prophets. The term *ša'arûrâ* occurs only twice in the Old Testament, the present passage and Jer. 5.30. Its precise referent is
unclear, but in both instances it is connected with the activity of
prophets who prophesy or 'walk' in *šeqer*. Jeremiah's charge is
that falsehood is the manner of life of these prophets, charac-
terizing the way in which they carry out the functions of their
office. The precise nature of this 'lie' will have to be determined by
the context, and the following sections will shed further light on
its interpretation. For the present it is at least evident that the term
refers to some action against Yahweh, since the result of the
prophets' functioning is that the wicked are strengthened and not
called to repentance. It is probable that the problem of false
confidence is at least part of what is involved here, since the people
apparently feel secure and therefore sense no need to repent.

The verse concludes:

> They have all become to me like Sodom,
>   and her (i.e., Jerusalem's) inhabitants like Gomorrah.

The tendency of commentators has been to see this reference to
the cities of Sodom and Gomorrah as an indication that Jeremiah
is placing the spotlight on the immorality of his opponents.
Rudolph notes that the Jerusalem prophets, instead of calling their
contemporaries to repentance, had, by their immorality, set a bad
example and become a source of corruption for the people. They
were thus no better than the people of Sodom and Gomorrah.[15]
Weiser also holds that the comparison is with the 'immoral inhabitants of Sodom and Gomorrah,'[16] and, after making a similar
point, Leslie notes that '. . . Sodom and Gomorrah were the classic

[13] *I & II Kings*, p. 36.
[14] *Überlieferungsgeschichtliche Studien* (Tübingen: Max Niemeyer Verlag,
1957), pp. 11f., 92.
[15] *Op. cit.*, p. 151.
[16] *Op. cit.*, p. 204; cf. also Hyatt, *op. cit.*, p. 991.

symbols of unspeakable wickedness and corruption.'[17] One obvious basis for such an interpretation is the fact that in v. 14 Jeremiah specifically charges the Jerusalem prophets with 'adultery'. As we have seen, this can refer to personal immorality, but the fact that there are passages in Hosea and Jeremiah in which the term is used in the context of a condemnation of apostasy shows that social immorality is not necessarily involved. That is, 'adultery' may refer to the unfaithfulness of the wife Jerusalem towards her husband Yahweh.[18]

The observation is perfectly correct that Sodom and Gomorrah serve as important symbols in the prophet's argument, and it is necessary to determine just what they are symbols of. The Genesis narratives know, of course, that Sodom (either mentioned alone or in connection with Gomorrah) was a wicked city, but the precise nature of this wickedness is difficult to ascertain.[19] For purposes of the present passage, however, the important observation is that most of the references to these cities beyond the book of Genesis hold them up as a kind of archetype of God's complete destruction of a people. This is the case, for example, in Isa. 1.9, where the Prophet asserts that it is only Yahweh's decision to allow a remnant to remain which has kept the destruction of Judah from being as complete as that of Sodom and Gomorrah.[20] And in the curse of Deuteronomy Israel herself is threatened with such a complete destruction if she commits the sin of breaking her covenant with Yahweh.[21] Thus Sodom and Gomorrah, though they probably call to mind the corruption of the people, are here primarily symbols of destruction. The activity of the prophets in Jerusalem, just as that of the former prophets of Samaria, leads to the destruction of the people. This is the nature of Yahweh's judgment.

[17] *Op. cit.,* p. 225.
[18] In Jer. 3.8f. there is an apparent reference to the exile of Israel after 722, a punishment brought out because of the nation's adultery.
[19] 13.13 (the men of Sodom are 'sinners against Yahweh'), 18.16–26 (the 'outcry' against them is great, their 'sin' is heavy, their inhabitants are 'evil'), 19.1–29.
[20] Similarly, D. Jones, 'Exposition of Isaiah Chapter One Verses Ten to Seventeen', *SJT* 18 (1965), pp. 457–59.
[21] Deut. 29.22 (cf. v. 25); for more examples of the cities as an archetype of destruction cf. Isa. 13.19; Jer. 49.18; 50.40; Zeph. 2.9; Amos 4.11. Beyond Genesis, where the character of the cities or their inhabitants is mentioned the reference is vague: Isa. 1.10; 3.9; Lam. 4.6; Ezek. 16.46–49.

Verse 15 continues this theme, although the terms 'wormwood' and 'poison water' are somewhat vague as descriptions of the way in which this destruction will come about. They are sometimes employed as descriptive terms in laments,[22] but are also used with reference to trouble sent by Yahweh as a punishment for sin.[23] All this will take place because 'from the Jerusalem prophets alienation has gone out to the whole land' (v. 15b). The actions of prophet and people have cut them off from the good will of their God.

The point of this comparison between the prophets of Samaria and those of Jerusalem is to make clear one of the causes of the coming fate of the land of Judah. The former had led the people of Israel astray, with the result that Yahweh had punished them through the destruction of their capital city and land. Now the people of Judah are being victimized by their prophets, and the result will be the same. In the following section Jeremiah develops further this indictment against the prophets.

The Charge Against the Prophets (16–22)

16   For thus says Yahweh of Hosts:
    Do not listen to the words of the prophets prophesying to you;
    they are filling you with vain hopes,[24]
        they speak a vision of their heart,
        not from Yahweh's mouth.

17   Saying continuously to those who reject Yahweh's word,[25]
        'You will have peace,'
    and to everyone who walks in the stubbornness of his heart
                    they say,
        'Evil will not come against you.'

18   For whoever has stood in Yahweh's council, let him see and hear
                    his word.
    Whoever has harkened to his word,[26] he has heard.

---

[22] Cf. Ps. 69.22; Lam 3.15, 19; in language tied in with that of the lamentations Amos 5.7 and 6.12 use these terms to describe the results to the weak of the perversion of justice.

[23] Jer. 9.11–15 (destruction and exile for breaking the law and serving the Baalim); 8.14 (destruction); Hos. 10.4; Deut. 29.17.

[24] Following the translation of Leslie, *op. cit.*, p. 226.

[25] LXX *apothoumenois ton logon kuriou* reflects a different pointing of the Hebrew: *limnaʾaśê dᵉbhar* rather than MT's *limnaʾṣay dibbēr*; cf. BHK³ mg. This must be correct, since the context requires that it be the 'rejectors' and not Yahweh who utter the following words.

[26] Absent in GSʰL; the immediate context calls for acceptance of the *Qᵉre*.

19 Behold, the tempest of Yahweh!
    Wrath has gone forth,
        a[27] twisting storm;
    It twists upon the head of the wicked.
20 The anger of Yahweh will not turn back
        until it has accomplished and established the
                                    purposes of his heart.
    In the end of days you will understand it perfectly.
21 I did not send the prophets,
        but they ran;
    I did not speak to them,
        but they prophesied.
22 If they had stood in my council,
        then they would have caused my people to hear my words,
        and caused them to turn back
            from their evil way and wicked deeds.

Verses 16–22 provide a rationale for Yahweh's judgment against the prophets, who have been largely responsible for what the people as a whole have done. The passage opens with an exhortation directed at the people: 'Do not listen to the words of the prophets prophesying to you. . .' The following general statement indicates why they are to follow this course of action: 'they are filling you with vain hopes. . .' The verb used here (*hbhl*) is infrequent in the Old Testament, but there are two occurrences which are particularly enlightening for the interpretation of the present passage. In II Kings 17.15 (in the midst of the Deuteronomist's interpretation of the causes of Samaria's fall) we are told that the people 'went after *hebel* and became *hebel*'. The context is one in which the people are accused of breaking the covenant commandments and serving other gods. In Jer. 2.5 the phrase occurs again verbatim; and again the context depicts the people as forsaking the God of the exodus and conquest (vv. 6f.) for other gods (vv. 8–13). Jeremiah's specific views concerning the 'falsehood of idolatry' will be touched upon below. For the present it must suffice to point out the gist of the prophet's general charge against his opponents: they are guilty of turning the people away from the living, powerful, effective God and causing them to place confidence in points of dogma or other deities, which by comparison are wholly ineffective and unsubstantial in character.

[27] Deletion of 'and' following the parallel passage 30.23.

The prophet now undertakes to explain more fully how his opponents have done this, asserting first of all that they '. . . speak a vision of their heart, not from Yahweh's mouth' (v. 16b). It cannot be the mere fact that the prophetic opponents speak visions (*ḥāzôn*) which is under attack here, since the vision was widely accepted as a legitimate form of Yahweh's revelation to the prophets. The books containing the prophecies of Isaiah, Obadiah, and Nahum all begin with a heading that describes what follows as the prophet's 'vision'. In I Sam. 3.1 'vision' is used in connection with the phrase 'word of Yahweh' and, as a prelude to Yahweh's call of Samuel, both were said to be rare (not given) in those days. Hos. 12.11 says that Yahweh has spoken to the prophets and multiplied their visions, and H.-W. Wolff sees this as a reference to the legitimate function of a chain of Northern prophets in making clear the guilt of the present situation.[28] Habakkuk is told by Yahweh to write down his vision (2.2f.), and Lamentations informs us that the fall of Jerusalem meant the destruction of the city, the exile of the nobility, the end of the law, and a situation in which the prophets no longer encountered a vision from Yahweh (2.9). In Ps. 89.20 Yahweh is said to have spoken by means of a vision to his 'faithful one', probably the king.[29] It seems then that the manner of receiving revelations from Yahweh is not here under attack. 'True' prophets may receive visions,[30] and the thing objected to in the prophetic opponents is not the fact *that* they receive them, but the *source* from which they come: their own hearts and not Yahweh's mouth.

Both the content of their preaching and the reception which it meets are evident in v. 17:

Saying continuously to those who reject Yahweh's word,
   'You will have peace,'
and to everyone who walks in the stubbornness of his heart they say,
   'Evil will not come against you.'

In Psalm 10 we hear of the wicked man who rejects Yahweh and thinks, 'There is no God' (vv. 3f.), who rejects him and says in his heart, 'You (i.e., Yahweh) will not call to account.' The psalmist's

---

[28] *Op. cit.,* p. 279.
[29] Cf. G. W. Ahlström, *Psalm 89,* pp. 101f.
[30] On the legitimacy of visions in the prophetic revelation cf. J. Lindblom, *op. cit.,* pp. 122–37.

opponent is seen to be basking in a kind of (false) security which, he feels, allows him to sin with impunity. He may do as he wishes, for Yahweh will not call him to account for his actions. It is against exactly this kind of sentiment, dealt with more fully in Chapter I, that Jeremiah speaks here. Though the people are guilty of rejecting Yahweh's injunctions and walking in the stubbornness of their own desires and intentions, they seem confident that their position is ultimately one of security. And it is precisely the prophets, who should be warning them that just the opposite is the case, who are found to be encouraging the people's activities with their crys: 'You will have peace . . . evil will not come against you!'

We gain some insight into the nature of the security which these prophets are proclaiming when we recognize that for Jeremiah 'peace' is for the most part taken to be the opposite of warfare or siege:

> Why do we sit still?
> Gather together, let us go into the fortified cities and perish there
> . . .
> We waited for peace,
>   but there was no good;
> for a time of healing,
>   but behold, terror.[31]

In the troubled political situation of Jeremiah's day it is no wonder that the major connotation of peace is that of security from warfare. And when the prophetic opponents preach such security, this places their message within the broad theme which was the subject of Chapter I.

Though the primary focus of Jeremiah's indictment is the activity of the prophets, a situation is presupposed in which the people have come to view their covenant with Yahweh as a one-sided affair in which security is guaranteed but little is demanded from them in return. This comes out in the prophet's use of the term *šᵉrirûth*, which in the Old Testament designates a very special kind of 'stubbornness', namely that in which a man turns away from following Yahweh and his commandments. Eight of the ten occurrences of this word are in Jeremiah, who identifies those who

---

[31] 8.14f.; cf. also 12.5, 12; 14.13, 19; 15.5; 16.5f.; 25.36f.; 29.7, 11; 30.5; 33.6, 9; 43.12.

follow the stubbornness of their own hearts as the breakers of
Yahweh's covenant (11.8), those who forsake his law and go after
the Baals (9.12f.).[32] Deuteronomy 29.18 also makes the point that
such a person (described as a poison root within the community)
may well feel that he is secure in his actions: when he hears the
words of the curse, he blesses himself in his heart saying, 'Peace
(*šālôm*) will be to me when (*kî*) I walk in the stubbornness of my
heart.'

The following verses make it quite clear that it is the content of
these prophecies of peace which condemns those who utter them.

> For whoever has stood in Yahweh's council, let him see and hear his
>   word.
> Whoever has hearkened to his word, he has heard.

Two observations are important here. In the first place, it is an
inherent part of the office of prophet that the men who hold it are
privy to the decisions reached in Yahweh's council.[33] Amos
stressed this point when he said that Yahweh does nothing unless
he reveals his counsel to his servants the prophets (3.7). Yet we
must notice in the second place that every man who occupies the
office of prophet need not be in continuous contact with that
council. That this is so is evident from the narrative of I Kings 22,
where it is Micaiah rather than the four hundred who has been
made aware of Yahweh's real intentions in the matter at hand.
This is, presumably, neither because they were 'merely' cultic
prophets (were they? was Micaiah different from them in this
respect?) nor because they were not genuine prophets and therefore never spoke the truth, but rather because a message having to
do with *this particular situation* had been revealed to Micaiah and
not to them. To say that their advice to the kings was wrong is not
to issue against them a blanket condemnation, but is to say that in

---

[32] Cf. also 3.17; 7.24; 13.10; 16.12; 18.12.

[33] In an early article on this subject H. Wheeler Robinson pointed to a very
'realistic' feeling among the prophets that they were admitted to the heavenly
council of Yahweh and the 'sons of God' with whom he associated himself.
It was through this concrete relationship that they knew themselves to be
privy to the divine plans for Israel. Cf. 'The Council of Yahweh', *JTS* 45
(1944), pp. 151–57, and similarly, F. M. Cross, 'The Council of Yahweh in
Second Isaiah', *JNES* 12 (1953), pp. 274–77. For analogies to this conception
in certain acts within the Babylonian *akitu* festival, cf. E. C. Kingsbury, 'The
Prophets and the Council of Yahweh', *JBL* 83 (1964), pp. 279–86.

this given instance their oracles were without foundation in the intention of Yahweh.

Jeremiah is saying that had his opponents really stood in Yahweh's council, they would have seen something quite different from what they purport. They would have seen the wrath of Yahweh going forth as a fierce storm (v. 19). They would have seen that peace was an illusion, that Yahweh's decision to send judgment upon his people was firm:

The anger of Yahweh will not turn back
  until it has accomplished and established the purposes of his heart
  (v. 20)

This judgment fits well with Jeremiah's perspective on the seriousness of the current scene. The sins of the people are so ingrained that they are no longer able, even if they desired to do so, to repent.[34] Against such divine resoluteness, all proclamations of security and peace are both deceptive and ineffective. In the 'latter days' the people will understand that his message, and not that of his opponents, was correct (v. 20b).

Verse 21, which serves to reinforce this principal argument against the prophetic opponents, says two things about them: that though Yahweh did not send them they ran, and that though he did not speak to them they prophesied. Taken positively, we will notice that these are the very two elements which were crucial in Jeremiah's own call to be a prophet to the nations (1.5ff.), for in his vision he was informed that (from time to time?) Yahweh would send him to someone and command him to speak a certain message. The crucial thing in a prophetic call is the authority which lies behind it. In the case of Jeremiah Yahweh puts his words in the prophet's mouth (1.9). The prophet becomes, in a sense, Yahweh's mouth (15.19), and whoever listens to him hears the words of God (37.2).

The problem, then, is whether Jeremiah is denying the validity of his opponents' message on the grounds that they had received no call. My contention is that he is not doing this, but is instead centring his attack on the content of their message. The case of Hananiah (ch. 28) clearly indicates that it is the message of the opponents and not their office which is the object of criticism. In 28.15 Jeremiah says that Yahweh 'did not send' Hananiah with his

34 Cf. 2.22; 13.23 and the comments of G. von Rad, *Theology* II, pp. 216ff.

false message of peace, but it is worth noting that Jeremiah did not level this charge on the occasion of their first encounter. Hananiah was apparently a serious prophet, but his message was the wrong one for the present situation. This is confirmed by a look at other passages in which Jeremiah says of his opponents that Yahweh 'did not send' them: in 14.13–16 it is specifically stated that the content of their message is 'peace'; in 27.14f. it is security from Babylonian conquest; and in 29.9 Jeremiah contends against a message of peace which takes the form of a prediction that the exile will be short. Thus Jeremiah was not saying that the opponents were merely imposters, or even that every prophecy of peace is necessarily a lie. The crucial factor here is the content of their message, which has harped on the theme of peace without at the same time stressing the need for repentance.

The following verse again mentions the source of prophetic revelation:

> If they had stood in my council,
>> then they would have caused my people to hear my words,
>> and caused them to turn back
>>> from their evil way and wicked deeds.

The crucial criterion for judging the validity of the utterances of prophetic opponents is the relevance of the content of their message to the contemporary situation. As we have seen, Jeremiah's view of the Judeans of his day involved the judgment that they were guilty both of grave infractions of the covenant and of expecting that Yahweh, regardless of their unfaithfulness, was somehow still bound to protect them. In Jeremiah's eyes this attitude could not be further from the truth, and thus he was convinced that if his opponents really were privy to Yahweh's council, they would have proclaimed a message which, far from offering easy comfort, would have called the people to repentance. The 'falsehood' in which they walk resides precisely in their strengthening of this sense of security in an evil people (v. 14).[35]

---

[35] Kraus considers this such a serious charge that he speaks of it as a 'criterion' by which one may judge between true and false prophets; *Prophetie . . .*, pp. 33, 35, 40, 46. The problem with this is that there might be room for differences of opinion as to just what constitutes strengthening the hand of evildoers. For example, anyone who was convinced of the validity of Hananiah's message might be expected to consider Jeremiah a traitor (and some did!; cf. 38.4).

Yahweh and the Prophets (23–32)

23   Am I a God close at hand,
>   says Yahweh,
and not a God afar off?

24   Or does a man hide in secret places,
        and I do not see him?
>   says Yahweh.
Am I not filling the heavens and the earth?
>   says Yahweh.

25   I have heard what the prophets prophesying a lie in my name
have spoken, saying, 'I have dreamed! I have dreamed!'

26   How long? Is (my word)[36] in the heart of the prophets who
prophesy the lie and who prophesy the delusion of their hearts,

27   those who plan to cause my people to forget my name by their
dreams, which each recounts to his companion, just as their
fathers forgot my name by Baal?

28   The prophet who has a dream, let him recount the dream, and
he who has my word, let him faithfully speak my word.
     What has chaff in common with wheat?
>   says Yahweh.

29   Is it not so? My word is like fire.
>   says Yahweh,
like a hammer it shatters rock.

30   Therefore behold, I am against the prophets,
>   says Yahweh,
who steal my words from each other.

31   Behold, I am against the prophets,
>   says Yahweh,
who take their tongues and say, 'A prophetic oracle!'

32   Behold, I am against those who prophesy false dreams,
>   says Yahweh,
and recount them and lead my people astray with their lies and
their boastings;
and I did not send them and I did not commend them and they
do not at all profit this people
>   says Yahweh.

---

[36] The translation here is at best a guess informed by the context of the
sentences which follow. The difficulties which translators have had with this
verse stem from the presence of a double interrogative at the beginning and
the apparent incompleteness (lack of predicate nominative) of the sentence
which follows.

In this section Yahweh's relationship to the prophets is characterized first of all by his remoteness (v. 23). The main connotation of the term 'afar off' is one of physical separation by distance, but in the present context the stress would seem to be on the distance between Yahweh and the prophets and therefore on the difficulties inherent in their having access to him. This fits with the charge previously made (vv. 18, 22) that they do not stand in his council, i.e., in open access to his decisions.[37] In another passage, which employs the same two terms used here, Jeremiah charges that his opponents have Yahweh close in their mouths but far from their 'kidneys' (12.2),[38] and this dichotomy typifies the prophet's judgment about his opponents, who relate oracles and dreams accompanied by the easy words 'says Yahweh' (cf. v. 31), but from whose hearts there is nothing more distant than an awareness of the seriousness of Yahweh's demands upon his people.

A second characteristic of Yahweh's relationship to the prophets is summed up in the questions of v. 24. In another context Yahweh, speaking through his prophet Jeremiah, makes a similar statement: '. . . my eyes are upon all their ways; they are not hid from me and their iniquity is not concealed from my eyes' (16.17). On the one hand, Yahweh is far from these prophets, while on the other nothing can remain hidden from him against his will. The actions of the prophetic opponents may well fall within the familiar prophetic office, enabling them through oracles and dreams to lead the people astray (vv. 13, 32). But the true valuation of these actions is known to Yahweh, who presumably shares his judgment with his prophet Jeremiah.

Yahweh sees all the activities of the prophets: he hears their exclamation 'I have dreamed! I have dreamed!' This statement highlights the difficulties involved in evaluating their work. It is a striking fact that in only a very few cases within the Old Testament is the 'dream' (*ḥalôm*) disparaged as something insubstan-

[37] The contrast expressed in v. 23 is very important for Kraus. It is the baalim, the 'new gods' (Deut. 32.17) who are near, while Yahweh's council is afar off (Jer. 31.3; Isa. 55.8f.). Yahweh's word is not always present (18.18), but often stands over against his people in judgment, for he is not near them always as a 'patron of security', but remains free and hidden in his activity, *Prophetie* . . ., p. 47; cf. pp. 50, 69, 75, 94.

[38] In Hebrew thought the kidneys are associated with the 'heart' as 'an important centre of psychic and moral life in man', R. C. Dentan, 'Kidneys', *IDB*[3] (K–Q), pp. 9f.

tial.[39] For the most part it is simply assumed that the dream is a legitimate and effective means by which Yahweh communicates with men, the double assumption being that he sends both the dream itself and the power to interpret it (cf. Gen. 40.8; 41.16). Dreams may reveal information regarding the present situation,[40] future states of affairs,[41] or the promises of Yahweh to an individual.[42] Dreams are connected with prophecy as part of the prophet's endowment,[43] and men may turn to dreams expecting to hear from Yahweh.[44] Deuteronomy 13.1-6 is an important passage in this regard. Here the prophet and 'dreamer of dreams' are mentioned together. From God (v. 4b) they have the power to do signs and wonders, and therefore an alleged lack of a call can serve as no basis for questioning their carrying out of the tasks of their office. Their validity is rather to be judged on the basis of the content of their message, so that any exhortation to serve other gods brings with it automatic condemnation.[45] In Jer. 27 and 29 the same criterion holds, the prophet condemning his opponents (among whom are sometimes included 'dreamers', 27.9; 29.8) on the basis of the content of their proclamation. The general point to be recognized is that '. . . dreams are one of the legitimate channels by which God reveals his will to chosen individuals. . .'[46]

With reference to the prophets, however, this general point has often been qualified. J. Lindblom, for example, says: 'To have

[39] Isa. 29.7f. is the clearest case; cf. also Ps. 73.20; Job 20.8; Eccles. 5.2, 6; Zech. 10.2.

[40] Gen. 20 (Abimelech learns the true identity of Sarah) and 31 (Jacob earns a method for outwitting Laban).

[41] Gen. 37, 40, 41 (all Joseph); Judg. 7 (Gideon learns of his forthcoming success over the Midianites); Dan. 2.

[42] Gen. 28.12 (Jacob at Bethel); I Kings 3 (Solomon at Gibeon).

[43] Num. 12.6; Jer. 29.8; note the parallelism of prophets, dreams, visions, etc. in Jer. 27.9; Joel 3.1; I Sam. 28.6, 15; Deut. 13.1-6.

[44] I Sam. 28; cf. Job 33.15.

[45] 13.1-6 is Deuteronomic material belonging to the class of 'parenetic "laws"' which offer a broad thematic treatment of a subject without having a discernible basis in any old legal statute', G. von Rad, *Studies in Deuteronomy,* trans. D. Stalker (SBT, First Series, 9, 1953), p. 22. The passage, according to G. E. Wright, comes from the ninth century or after, i.e., from a time 'when false prophecy became a serious problem', *IB*, II, p. 419.

[46] I. Mendelsohn, 'Dream; Dreamer', *IDB* 1 (A–D), p. 868; cf. A. Johnson, *The Cultic Prophet in Ancient Israel* (2nd ed. rev.; Cardiff: University of Wales Press, 1962), pp. 46ff. Mendelsohn points out that dreams were a common mode of revelation in the Ancient Near East, examples of revelatory dreams being known from Babylonia and Ugarit. On Keret's dream cf. also P. R. Ackroyd, 'Some Notes on the Psalms', *JTS*, NS 17 (1966), p. 395.

dreams that came true was also part of the prophetic endowment. . . But the classical prophets did not attach value to
dreams.'[47] Even those who do not make such a blanket statement
tend to see Jeremiah as something of an anomaly, since in distinction from both earlier (cf. Gen. and Num. 12.6) and later (cf. Joel
3.1) times he rejects dreams as a means of Yahweh's revelation.[48]
Leslie's comment on the passage under discussion represents the
epitome of this view: 'Here we see Jeremiah take a significant step
forward, away from the irrational and toward the rational.'[49]

Basic to this scholarly judgment that Jeremiah discounts the
validity of dreams is a contrast of *external forms,* a contrast of
dream and word. Lindblom furnishes us with a statement of
principle on the matter: 'Dreams can be interesting to tell and to
listen to, but they have nothing to do with Yahweh's word. They
are empty and erroneous, and powerless, while the divine word is
true and mighty.'[50] The basic mistake here would seem to be that
of seeing something inherently inferior in the dream *form.* Such a
tendency is especially pronounced with reference to vv. 28f.
According to Rudolph the contrast set out in the first of these
verses resolves itself into something like the equation, dream:
word of Yahweh : : chaff: wheat. Weiser also stresses the fact that
'God's word is an active, living force, which comes over the
prophets from outside and crushes every opposition'. It is in this
powerful intervention from the outside that Jeremiah recognizes
the 'reality and genuineness of the divine word' in his own
thoughts and feelings (cf. 1.6ff.; 10.19; 23.9). Thus, 'only he who
is from the truth hears God's voice; in inner, unpretentious
veracity, which will be muddied by no sort of egotistical subordi-
nate ideas, Jeremiah sees one of the most decisive criteria which
distinguish the true from the false prophets.'[51] But the real problems of using such a criterion of inner certainty in the evaluation
of a prophet's veracity are more than evident in the case of Hananiah, examined above. Further, though commentators make much
of the inherent power of Yahweh's 'word', we may assume that
this power was not especially apparent in the unfulfilled threats of

[47] *Op. cit.,* p. 201.
[48] So Rudolph; cf. Johnson, *op. cit.,* p. 46.
[49] *Op. cit.,* p. 227.
[50] *Op. cit.,* p. 201; Johnson speaks of 'mere dreams', *op. cit.,* p. 46.
[51] *Op. cit.,* pp. 210f.; cf. also Hyatt, *op. cit.,* p. 994.

violence and destruction which Jeremiah uttered over a period of three decades before the first fall of Jerusalem (cf. 20.7ff.).

Closer to the truth is the observation that a major drawback of these dreams was their bad effect upon the people. Rudolph sees the dreams being rejected not only because of their origin, but also because of their effect, namely, they cause the people to forget Yahweh (v. 27). Weiser concurs, noting that the dreams have exactly the opposite effect from what a proclamation of the true word would have: they cause God to be forgotten rather than remembered. We should note, however, that this observation really has nothing to do with the dream form itself, and in no way necessitates a blanket condemnation of that form. The dreams mislead not because of what they *are*, but because of what they *contain*. Even a false word of Yahweh could have the same effect.

Verses 26f. point their finger at a prophesied lie which has caused the people to forget Yahweh's name. The question is, what is the content of this lie? The term 'lie' is here used in parallel with the phrase 'the delusion of their heart', and Jer. 14.14 provides some insight into the connotation which the latter had for the prophet. There it is said that Yahweh did not send, command or speak to the prophets, yet they continued to speak false visions, worthless divination, and 'the delusion of their heart'. And the preceding verse gives us an explicit statement of the content of the message so described, as speaking in Yahweh's name these opponents are pictured as saying: '. . . I will give you assured peace in this place.' The delusion thus refers to the sense of security under which the people exist, and for the prophet it is axiomatic that a people under the influence of such a 'delusion' will not return to and honour the demand which Yahweh makes of them (cf. 8.5). They have, in fact, 'forgotten' Yahweh, which in reality means that they have embarked upon a course of action different from that desired by him (cf. 3.21). Specifically, this forgetting of Yahweh may involve going after other gods,[52] and in 13.25 Yahweh says through Jeremiah that the people's sin will bring about their destruction because '. . . you forgot me and trusted in the lie.' We may simply note that elsewhere in Jeremiah 'trusting in the lie' has specific reference to a false confidence in

[52] 18.15; 23.27 (Baal); cf. also 2.32 (much of ch. 2 is concerned with idolatry).

slogans of security (7.4, 8) and to the equally groundless confidence that the exile will be a short one (28.15; 29.31). The people have thus entered onto a new course of action, a course which is analogous to one adopted in a previous time of Israel's history, the fathers' forgetting of Yahweh's name under the influence of Baal.

The traditional views of vv. 28f. have already been discussed. The problem with them is that there seems to be no disparaging tone in the reference to dreams in v. 28a. Both dream and word are apparently assumed to be valid. Thus the chaff-wheat analogy of v. 28b is between dreams *and* words which lead the people astray (vv. 26f.; cf. vv. 13, 32) and dreams *and* words which call a wayward people to repentance and responsibility. It is the latter which have the power of fire and of a hammer which shatters rock (cf. Isa. 55.10f.). These verses in effect state a kind of norm for judging the legitimacy of the prophets. Since they do not conform to it, the condemnation of vv. 30–32 is justified.

In the final three verses of the section, then, judgment is pronounced against the prophetic opponents. Three specific grounds for Yahweh's condemnation are mentioned: they steal oracles from one another, they take it upon themselves to speak in his name, and they prophesy false dreams which lead the people astray. Following the line of interpretation adopted above, we should view these statements not as a condemnation of the forms themselves, but rather of a common abuse of them. A dream may in fact contain a revelation from Yahweh, but there are also false dreams which do not (v. 32). The general charge is that Yahweh has not sent these opponents and that they have led the people astray with their own lies. This point is substantiated by calling attention to the origin of what they say and dream. Their oracles are the products of their own tongues (v. 31), or have been taken over from the utterances of companions. By their content they are known to be false: they harp on the theme 'peace', when the historical situation to which they are addressed is one in which Yahweh is standing over against his people in judgment.

The 'Burden' of Yahweh (33–40)

33   And when this people or a prophet or a priest asks you saying,
      'What is the burden of Yahweh?', you will say to them, 'You

34 are the burden,[53] and I will abandon you, says Yahweh.' And
    the prophet and the priest and the people who says, 'Burden of
35 Yahweh', I will punish that man and his house. Thus you will
    say, each to his neighbour and his brother, 'What has Yahweh
36 answered and what has Yahweh said?' And you will no longer
    remember the burden of Yahweh, for each man's word will be
    the burden, and you twist the words of the living God, Yahweh
37 of hosts, our God. Thus you will say to the prophets, 'What
38 did Yahweh answer you and what did Yahweh say?' But if you
    say, 'Burden of Yahweh', therefore thus says Yahweh, 'Because
    you spoke this word, "Burden of Yahweh", and I sent to you
39 saying, "Do not say burden of Yahweh", therefore behold I
    will surely lift you and abandon you and the city, which I gave
40 to you and your fathers, from before my face. And I will make
    you an eternal reproach and an eternal insult, which will not be
    forgotten.'

Commentators tend to regard this passage as an appendix to the
preceding collection of oracles against the prophets, v. 33 being a
genuine utterance of Jeremiah and vv. 34–40 reflecting a legalistic
misunderstanding and misrepresentation of the word-play involving the term *massā*'.[54]

Leaving aside the question of the 'genuineness' of the passage,
the development of thought is as follows: Verse 33 mirrors a
situation in which the prophet is consulted to learn if he has
received a word from Yahweh regarding the current situation (cf.
21.1ff.). The meaning of the action described revolves around a
word-play on *massā*', which may refer either to a 'load' or 'burden'
carried by a beast (Ex. 23.5) or a man (Num. 4.15ff.), or to an
'oracle' of Yahweh (Isa. 15.1). The people ask for an oracle, but
Jeremiah's response ('You are the burden. . . .') brings home the
point that there is to be no other word from Yahweh than the
announcement of judgment he has been bringing them all along.
Yahweh's determination to enter into judgment against his people
is final. Since the oracles of 23.9ff. have all along been holding the
prophets particularly responsible for this state of affairs, it seems

[53] Following Greek, Old Latin, and Vulgate. This reading fits the context
better than MT's rather strange 'What burden?' and can be derived from the
consonantal text in several ways. Cf. Giesebrecht, *op. cit.*, p. 132, and Rudolph,
op. cit., p. 154.

[54] E.g., Rudolph, *op. cit.*, pp. 155–57; Weiser, *op. cit.*, p. 212; Leslie,
op. cit., pp. 250ff., 320f.

fitting to view Lam. 2.14 as a *post eventum* commentary on their contribution to the catastrophe which befell Judah:

> Your prophets have seen for you vainly (*šāw'*) and
> worthlessly.
> They have not revealed your guilt to restore your fortune,
> but have seen for you oracles (*mas'ôth*) vain (*šāw'*)
> and enticing.

In the context of a great lamentation over the fall of Judah, this passage is a cry of anguish and betrayal against the prophets who misled the people. How had they done this? By not calling the people's guilt into account, and thus presumably fostering the notion that peace would prevail. This is the same picture of the activity of the prophetic opponents that we have been encountering all along.

Besides the basic word-play in v. 33, there is perhaps further irony in the fact that *massā'* often designates a specific kind of oracle, the oracle against a foreign nation.[55] Jeremiah, confronted by the question, 'Is there an oracle (against our enemies)?' retorts, 'You are the oracle (burden).' That is to say, the oracle, traditionally directed against Judah's enemies, is now directed back upon herself.[56]

Verse 34 goes on to say that anyone who presumes to utter a prophetic oracle will be punished. The remainder of the passage informs us that what has been spoken previously is sufficient guidance for the people (vv. 35, 37), and even that has been perverted (v. 36). Verses 38–40 expand v. 34 by extending in both space (the 'city' is now included, as well as individuals) and time (the judgment is to be everlasting) the punishment directed to those who presume to speak an oracle of Yahweh.

The passage as a whole is thus based on a conception of the activity of Jeremiah's opponents which is in harmony with the preceding verses. Proceeding from this recognition, a guess can be made regarding its growth in the on-going development of the traditional materials associated with the prophet Jeremiah. From the prophet himself comes at least the basic idea that Yahweh's judgment against the people is final, and that the blame for this

---

[55] Cf. Nahum 1.1; Isa. 13.1; 14.28; 15.1; 19.1, 21.11, 13; 23.1.

[56] One recalls Amos 1–2, where a series of oracles against foreign nations culminates in an extended attack against Israel herself.

resides primarily in the activity of his opponents. This insight then provides the basis for a subsequent generalization to the effect that prophecy itself is dead. One cannot know for certain when such an interpretation might appropriately have arisen, though it may be suggested that it need not be as late as the decline of prophecy following the restoration. If those responsible for the generalization were ignorant of Ezekiel's activity, or if they lived in the years between Ezekiel and Second Isaiah, we might even arrive at a date as early as the exile. The picture which ch. 29 gives of religious life among the exiles may even provide us with an appropriate historical situation, for there we see a people who had twisted Yahweh's former words listening again to prophets who do not speak the truth. For Jeremiah the words of such men were more a 'burden' than an 'oracle'. Certainly a group that had learned no more from the catastrophe of recent history than these men had must have seemed to him strangely dead both to the centre of the nation's theological traditions and to current historical events. One can readily imagine the prophet wondering whether the institution of prophecy was itself not about to die.

So we have seen that the main issue in 23.9–40 is not that of the morality or inauthenticity of the prophets, but is rather the content of the message with which they are leading the people astray. It was a message which encouraged them to feel secure even in their irresponsibility towards Yahweh's demands upont hem. It was pre-eminently the wrong message for the present historical situation, a message of peace and security in the face of what Jeremiah saw to be the continuing power of the Neo-Babylonian empire. The content of this series of oracles is thus quite in harmony with that of the narratives of concrete cases of Jeremiah's polemic against prophetic opponents dealt with in the preceding chapter.

IV

EARLY ORACLES AGAINST THE PROPHETS

WE must now turn to six occurrences of the term *šeqer* in the collections of oracles immediately preceding and following the prose sermon of 7.1–8.3. In four of these the term forms part of a polemic directed against Judah's religious leaders, the prophets and priests (5.31; 6.13 = 8.10; 8.8), while the remaining two illustrate its application to a broader social situation (9.2, 4). It is commonly felt that these chapters come from the earlier periods of Jeremiah's prophetic activity. Rudolph, for example, sees chs. 1–6 as a series of oracles stemming from the time of king Josiah, while the oracles of chs. 7–20 are for the most part from the time of Jehoiakim.[1] While the aim of the present inquiry is not to make an exhaustive study of chs. 4–6 and 8–9, a few general comments are necessary to provide a background for discussing the specific oracles that are of interest to us.

We note first of all that the chapters flanking ch. 7 are made up mostly of short oracles exhibiting Westermann's two-part pattern of organization: a charge or accusation directed against the people, which provides the basis for a proclamation of judgment. In every instance the term *šeqer* appears in the section of the oracle which develops the charge. In the second place, it has been commonly recognized that chs. 4–6 form a complex of oracles concerned with the theme of an enemy approaching from the North, and though the directional emphasis is not quite so strong, threat of conquest is predominant in chs. 8–9 as well.[2] In both groups of chapters one frequently encounters the language of lamentation in connection with the threat of coming destruction (cf. 4.8; 6.26; 8.14f., 18–23; 9.9, 16–19). The chapters are thus in basic agreement both as to the nature and the immediacy of Yahweh's judgment against his people.

---

[1] *Op. cit.*, pp. 1, 13f., 50f.
[2] Cf. 8.10, 14–16 (where an attack from the North is implied); 9.9f., 19, 22.

The question is now that of the nature of the indictment which
Jeremiah brought against the people. If judgment is certain, what
is its basis? To answer this question we will have to examine some
of the more important accusations which the prophet directs
against the people in this group of oracles.

5.30–31 stands outside the structure of the preceding portion of
that chapter,[3] and forms an accusation addressed specifically
against the prophets and priests:

> A dreadful and a horrible thing has happened in the land:
> the prophets prophesied in falsehood,
>   and the priests rule according to their hands,
>   and my people love it so. . . .

The curious thing here is that, while the prophet seems to be
equating the actions of these officials with the dreadful happenings
in the land, the term *šammā* normally refers to the dreadful event
of destruction which is Yahweh's punishment sent against a sinful
people.[4] If this is the case, then the lie being proclaimed by the
prophets is seen as being in itself a destructive force. There is
widespread disagreement over the proper way to translate the
phrase describing the priests' activity,[5] though whatever translation is adopted the issue seems to resolve itself into a dispute over
the proper basis of priestly authority. It is Yahweh who should
have authority in his hand and the priests should thus proclaim his
Torah, but Jeremiah finds that they '. . . give instruction as it suits
them by virtue of their own authority'.[6] Thus in this short accusation the term *šeqer* is used to describe the tendency of religious

[3] Note the repetition of the refrain in vv. 9 and 29.

[4] Cf. Jer. 2.15; 4.7; 18.16; 19.8; 25.9, 11, 18, 38; 29.18; 42.18; 46.19; 48.9;
49.13, 17; 50.3, 23; 51.29, 37, 41, 43.

[5] Much of the ambiguity resides in the verb, which I have taken as coming
from *rdh* I ('tread, rule'; cf. Weiser), but which Hyatt, *op. cit.* (following Duhm)
takes from *rdh* II ('. . . they scrape into their own hands') and Rudolph from
yrh III ('And the priests teach at their own fist'; cf. Leslie, 'and the priests
instruct according to their own authority').

[6] Rudolph, *op. cit.*, p. 41. Leslie and Weiser concur in this judgment: 'Here
religion stands no more in the service of God, of the one Lord, but was
degraded to a human transaction'. Weiser, *op. cit.*, p. 50. In line with this
interpretation Rudolph asserts that *baššeqer* serves here as 'a kind of personification' (p. 42) for *baba'al* (cf. 2.8; 23.13): the 'god of lies Baal' thus comes
to the fore as the source of the prophets' revelation. He adopts this position
in explicit opposition to J. Milgrom, who argued that the change of wording
between 2.8 (*nibbe' ûbabba'al*) and 5.31 (*nibbe' û baššeqer*), when seen in the light
of the 'catalogue of charges' of 5.26–28, indicates that the prophets' period of

leaders to reject, ignore, or at least not seek the authority of Yahweh over their activities, a tendency which the prophet sees as being in itself destructive in the people's life.

The accusation of 6.6b–7 is couched in the general terminology of social oppression, the imagery arising from Jeremiah's recognition of 'the basically corrupted character of the city'.[7] The prophet becomes somewhat more specific, however, in the following oracle:

> To whom will I speak and warn and they will listen?
> Behold, their ears are uncircumcised,
>   and they are not able to give attention;
> behold, the word of Yahweh has become to them a reproach,
>   and they do not take pleasure in it (6.10).

The people have apparently refused to heed Yahweh's word, here certainly the message which Jeremiah has felt compelled to convey to them. This verse is sometimes taken to be our earliest indication that Jeremiah was subjected to the derisive mocking of his fellow countrymen because of the message he proclaimed,[8] and if nothing else it indicates that what he considered to be the just demands of Yahweh upon them were not being heeded. Along these lines it is interesting to note the prevalence of three words in the expressions which these chapters give to the accusation against the people: *tôrāh* (6. [16f.], 19; 8.8; 9.12), *dābhār* (6.10, 19; 8.9), and *mišpaṭ* (8.7).

Of major interest is the accusation directed against prophet and priest in 6.13–15 (=8.10–12):

> For from the least of them to the greatest
>   each seeks a large profit,

---

idolatry was behind and 'the *šeqer* referred to is purely moral in character' ('The Date of Jeremiah, Chapter 2', *JNES* 14 [1955], pp. 67f.). 5.31 thus dates after Josiah's reform. It will suffice to suggest (in support of Rudolph against Milgrom) that it is not clear either that idolatry ceased to be a problem after 621 or that 5.30f. stands in such a close causal connection to the preceding portions of that chapter. It should be mentioned, however, that it is possible to understand this verse as referring to the prophets' rejection of Yahweh's authority without subscribing to Rudolph's 'personification' theory.

[7] Weiser, *op. cit.*, p. 54.
[8] So Rudolph, and Hyatt, *op. cit.*, p. 859. One inevitably recalls the lament of 20.7ff.

and from prophet to priest
   each acts falsely;
and they healed the fracture of my people superficially,
   saying, 'Peace, peace,'
      but there is no peace.
They are put to shame,
   for they committed an abomination;
they were neither ashamed,
   nor did they know how to feel humiliated.

Here the prophetic and priestly proclamation of 'peace' is equated with the phrase 'do a lie', and we notice the apparent difference between the sin of the people and that of the religious leaders. The possibility immediately suggests itself that the latter's preaching of an easy security has amounted to a relinquishing of their proper task (that of calling the people to return to the covenant obligations), making them ultimately responsible for the continuance of the sins of the former.

The term used to express the people's brokenness (*šebher*, 'fracture') is the same as that used in 4.6 and 6.1 to describe the coming 'destruction' at the hands of the enemy from the North. The situation corresponds to Amos 6.6, since Amos too saw 'destruction' of the land as an imminent but not yet accomplished punishment of a sinful people. Thus in 6.14 (=8.11) we are to understand Jeremiah as condemning the activity of religious leaders who are glossing over the reality of the imminent destruction of the land in such a way that the people can go on as before, confident of the fact that Yahweh will protect them come what may. Here we are again confronting the phenomenon of excessive confidence in a false conception of security examined in Chapter I. The prophets are seen to be false precisely because the message which they proclaim is false. They proclaim peace,[9] but the mere

[9] On the nature of the 'peace' which they proclaim cf. above, pp. 58f. On the absolute antithesis between *šālôm* ('complete harmony between friends and victory in war against enemies') and *šebher* ('an infringement upon the whole, which is peace') cf. J. Pedersen, *Israel: Its Life and Culture* I-II (London: Oxford University Press, 1926), pp. 311ff. Pedersen has also shown how the earlier dynamic conception of peace came through the influence of Canaan and the monarchy to be regarded as a passive kind of security for the status quo which was 'the opposite of fighting and strenuous effort', p. 329. Something of the latter seems characteristic of the conception of peace as proclaimed by the prophetic opponents.

proclamation does not make it so and in so far as their proclamation serves to blunt the sensitivities and cloud the vision of the people regarding the seriousness of their situation their falsehood takes on an absolutely destructive quality.[10]

The root *bwš*, usually translated 'be ashamed', seems in its basic meaning to refer to that sense of uneasiness which arises due to the uncertainty of a specific situation.[11] Similarly, the verb can be used to designate the people's reaction to military destruction (II Kings 19.26; Jer. 51.51), and it should be noticed that the connection of 'being ashamed' with the recognition of one's sin is late and infrequent (Jer. 31.19; Ezra 9.6). What of the passage at hand? The RSV translates the first phrase of v. 15 as a question ('Were they ashamed when they committed abomination?'), but MT has no interrogative and seems to demand a translation on the order of that offered above.[12] This is to be understood in terms of a contrast between Yahweh's attitude (judgment against the people: 15a – 'they are put to shame, for . . .'; 15b*b* – 'therefore they shall fall . . .') and that of the people (15b*a* – neither shamed nor humiliated), who do not sense the fact that their actions are upsetting the established order of their relationship with Yahweh. There is an obvious tie-in here with their false sense of security, of having guaranteed peace regardless of their deeds, and we notice how well this judgment fits with the insistence of this whole group of oracles that the people have abandoned or refused to heed Yahweh's word, law, and ordinances.

In terms of this particular polemic against his opponents, then, *šeqer* refers to the content of the message by which the prophet himself is known to be false. The message was one of peace, and its effect would have been the strengthening of the sense of security under the shadow of which the people lived. Several other passages where something of the same idea is expressed (though

---

[10] Rudolph contends that the falsehood of the prophets is not a matter of 'personal mendacity.' Rather '. . . they do not recognize the signs of the times, so that their instruction, perhaps given in good faith, does not correspond to the actual circumstances . . .'; *op. cit.*, p. 45.

[11] Cf. Judg. 3.25; Jer. 14.3f.; II Sam. 19.6f. (the confusion of David's army over the fact that what in the normal order of things should have been a cause for celebration has unaccountably become a cause for mourning), Joel 1.11.

[12] Reading *mikkālēm* for *haklîm*, following the parallel passage in 8.12. Cf. the similar translations of Rudolph and Weiser.

not necessarily employing the term *šeqer*) come to mind. One is Micah 3.5–12:[13]

> Thus says Yahweh against the prophets
> who are causing my people to err,
> who having something to eat cry 'Peace,'
> but declare war on him who puts nothing in their mouths.
> Therefore it shall be night to you without vision. . . .
>
> . . .
> Hear this, now, O heads of the house of Jacob. . . .
> . . .
> building Zion with blood,
> and Jerusalem with wrong.
> Its heads judge for a bribe,
> and its priests instruct for a price,
> and its prophets divine for silver,
> and they support themselves on Yahweh saying,
> 'Is not Yahweh in our midst?
> Evil will not come upon us!' (5–6a, 9, 10f.)

Again, it is obvious that the message of the prophets is one which stresses the people's guaranteed security in their land and city, and Micah counters their assertion with the oracle against Jerusalem with which this passage ends (v. 12). G. Quell has pointed out that we ought not to take the fact that prophets are here pictured as plying their trade for hire as being the main object of Micah's attack. The receipt of an honorarium for an oracle delivered can be assumed to have been a legitimate custom (cf. I Sam. 9.7f.; II Kings 8.9; Jer. 40.5). Sociologically, this can be taken as simply a 'hard fact', since the prophets had to live somehow. Thus for Micah the decisive thing was not that these prophets accepted payment for their services but that, swayed by economic influences, they ceased to be prophets without ceasing to act and speak like them. Theirs is a private opportunism. They have a message of salvation which can be bought (v. 11), and because of this are out of touch with what Micah takes to be the true seriousness of the present situation.[14]

One other passage should be dealt with here, Jer. 14.13–16:

And I said, 'Ah, Lord Yahweh, behold the prophets who speak to

---

[13] Cf. A. S. van der Woude, 'Micah in Dispute with the Pseudo-Prophets', *VT* 19 (1969), pp. 244–60, who concludes that the message of Micah's opponents had its basis in the Sinai and Zion traditions.

[14] *Op. cit.*, pp. 116ff.

them, "You will not see the sword, and famine will not be to you, for I will give you certain peace in this place." ' And Yahweh spoke to me, 'The prophets are prophesying a lie in my name. I did not send them and I did not command them and I did not speak to them, for they are prophesying to you a false vision and divination and nothingness and the deceit of their heart. Therefore thus says Yahweh against the prophets prophesying in my name and I did not send them, and they say, "Sword and famine will not be on this land"; these prophets will die by sword and famine. And the people to whom they prophesy will be cast out into the streets of Jerusalem before the famine and the sword, and there will not be anyone burying them – they, their wives, their sons, and their daughters; and I will pour out their evil upon them.'

According to Rudolph, the emphasis in this passage is upon the fact that the prophets do not have the authority from Yahweh that they claim to have. They lack the very thing 'which constitutes the true prophets; the ability to distinguish between their own thoughts and the divine inspiration. . . .'[15] What does the passage tell us about the prophetic opponents? It tells us, first of all, that they proclaim a message of 'peace', and, secondly, that Jeremiah is convinced that Yahweh has not authorized them to do so. On the historian's relative scale of valuation the first of these comes closest to being a 'fact' of history, while the second is obviously the prophet's interpretation of a certain set of 'facts' or a particular situation which he encounters. In the verses immediately preceding this paragraph (10f.) we encounter Yahweh's condemnation of the people for their sins, concluding with a command to the prophet not to intercede on their behalf and an announcement of the approaching destruction. In this context v. 13 looks like an indirect intercession by Jeremiah on the people's behalf, in which he puts the blame for the people's straying upon the prophets and their *šeqer* message. They have not repented because the prophets have continually preached their doctrine of security and they have therefore seen no need to 'amend their ways and their doings' (7.3). It is clear that the content of their message is a more certain and more important criterion for judging the genuineness or falsity of the prophetic opponents than is any alleged lack of a general call or a specific commission; more certain because it is capable of at least a measure of judgment in the light of the current

[15] *Op. cit.,* p. 101.

historical situation, more important because the authority of a prophet is not a neutral or an independent issue but becomes important only in the case of conflicting claims.

Finally, a word about Jeremiah 5.12f.:

> They have denied Yahweh,
>   and have said, 'He will not (do anything),
> no evil will come upon us,
>   and we will not see sword and famine.
> The prophets will become wind,
>   and there is no word in them;
> thus it will be done to them.'

One might say that these verses represent the other side of the coin from the passages just cited. For here we see men who are convinced of the validity of the opponents' message of peace asserting that the words of the prophets of doom will prove as empty as wind. The sense of the passage is not that Yahweh is inactive or ineffective within the realm of human events, but rather that he will not act in a certain way, namely in the sending of sword and famine against his own people. Jeremiah interprets this sense of security as a 'denial' of Yahweh.

The next element of the accusation developed in ch. 6 comes in vv. 16–17, 19b where we have pictured the people's rejection of two specific exhortations:

> Thus says Yahweh,
> Stand on the roads and look,
>   and ask for the ancient paths where the good way is,
> and walk in it
>   and find rest for your souls.
> But they said, 'We will not walk.'
> And I set watchmen over you:
>   'Heed the voice of the trumpet!'
> But they said, 'We will not give attention.'
>   . . .
> they did not give heed to my words
>   and they rejected my law.

The theme struck here, that of the people's refusal to repent, is a recurring one in the chapters under discussion.[16]

J. P. Hyatt, in an article 'Torah in the Book of Jeremiah', lists

---

[16] Cf. 6.15, 16f., 27–30; 8.4–7, 12; 9.4 (LXX).

this as one of the passages in which the prophet indicates his understanding of what the law *is* (as contrasted with passages like 8.8 which show his conception of what is not properly law).[17] Hyatt notes that at first glance the 'my words' and 'my law' of v. 19 seem to be parallel (as in Isa. 1.10), but that upon further investigation this proves not to be the case. In structure the passage takes the form of a short review of Israel's history (cf. 2.1–13) in which the rejection of the ancient paths is followed by the rejection of the watchmen. The latter are obviously the prophets, to whom v. 19 refers when it says that the people have not heeded 'my words'. 'My law' must therefore refer back to the ancient paths, by which expression the prophet intends to designate the Mosaic period with its disobedience to Yahweh's true revelation (cf. 2.2ff.; 7.22ff.). Jeremiah's conception of the law is further clarified in 7.5f., 9, 22f., which show us '. . . that Jeremiah considered as the true torah of Yahweh the ethical requirements and the prohibition against the worship of other gods which has been given to Israel in the desert by Moses. With this is contrasted the ritualistic requirements put forward by the priests (cf. 6.20) and the dependence upon the existence of the temple for salvation.'[18] Though we may accept Hyatt's analysis of the structure of this passage, we must differ with at least some aspects of his interpretation of it, for at issue here is not a supposed cleavage between ethical and cultic action, but the refusal of the people to break away from their static conception of the security which their heritage offers them and heed the new word which Yahweh is speaking to them in their present historical situation. It seems likely that in a passage like 6.13ff. Jeremiah is chiding the priests and prophets precisely because they failed in their function of instructing the people in the Torah, the covenant obligations laid upon them in their relationship to Yahweh. What is criticized here is the declared defiance of a people which refuses to tread the right path when it has a chance to do so. The reference to the people's past calls to mind the fact that they would have prospered had they remained faithful to Yahweh, but they did not. Their defiance prepares the way for the coming destruction (vv. 18f.). The line of argumentation is in many ways similar to that employed in 7.1–15.

[17] *JBL* 60 (1941), pp. 389ff.
[18] *Ibid.*, p. 392.

The first oracle of chapter 8 develops its accusation in two parts. In the first of these (8.4–7) Jeremiah uses a 'commonplace example' of men erring and correcting their errors, the point of which is that while occasional error is understandable, perpetual error is inconceivable. Yet the latter is precisely what characterizes Judah in the prophet's time. In v. 7 the prophet moves from the sphere of daily life to that of animal life. When we remember that what we ascribe to 'instinct or a law of nature' the ancient world-view understands as the response to a divine command, we see that Jeremiah is again setting up a contrast, this time between the birds who follow the divine regulation and a Judah which does not (cf. 5.22f.; Isa. 1.3).[19] Verse 7 concludes:

> but my people do not know
> the judgment of Yahweh.

Thus in 8.4–7 we have painted for us the picture of a people who reject their relationship to Yahweh by abandoning the obligations which he has laid upon them (cf. 4.22).

In the second part of the accusation (8.8–9) the focus of attention again narrows to the leaders of the people:

> How do you say, 'We are wise,
> and the law of Yahweh is with us'?
> Indeed! Behold the false pen of the scribes
> has made it into a lie.[20]
> The wise are ashamed,
> they are filled with terror and seized;
> behold, they rejected the word of Yahweh,
> and what wisdom is in them?

Hyatt assumes that the Torah spoken of in these verses is a written one, which is being contrasted with the spoken 'word' of the prophets. He thinks that Jeremiah began his ministry a decade after Josiah's reform, and thus probably had Deuteronomy (though possibly also parts of the Covenant Code, H, and P) in mind when he uttered this judgment. The scribes mentioned here must have been more than secretaries and copyists, they must 'to some degree' have been interpreters and makers of Torah. Thus

[19] Rudolph, *op. cit.*, pp. 60f; cf. Weiser, *op. cit.*, p. 71.
[20] So Rudolph (following Duhm, Cornill), Weiser, Leslie, RSV. The obscurity of LXX indicates that the uncertainty concerning the exact translation of this passage is a long-standing one.

Jeremiah is against the written Torah because it does not agree
with the word of Yahweh given through the prophets.[21] One
trouble with this interpretation, however, is that the scribal office
before the exile was a secular one. The priestly scribal class
(guardians of the Law) 'had their origins in the condition of the
Exile'.[22] We must conclude that 8.8 refers not so much to overt
priestly perversion of the law by wilful interpretations of it, as to
the perhaps covert perversion of Yahweh's demands at the hands
of officialdom. As one of the highest of civil officials, the scribe
would have some responsibility in the proclaiming and carrying
out of royal decrees, and the implication here is that both he and
his master have been guilty of ignoring the demands of Yahweh in
their conduct of the affairs of the kingdom. Taking the context as
a whole, Jeremiah is hardly rejecting the written Torah in favour
of his prophetic word, but is charging the people with having
rejected both Yahweh's Torah and his word (cf. 6.16–19; 8.7).
The falsification (*šeqer*) of the law depicted here is thus closely
allied to that easy attitude towards Yahweh's covenant obligations
already discussed in Chapter I.[23]

The next elements of accusation (8.10–12 repeat 6.13ff.) that
we encounter come in 9.1–2, 3–5 :

1   O that I had in the desert a wanderer's lodge,
  and I would abandon my people
   and depart from them;
  for all are adulterers,
   an assembly of treacherous ones.

[21] 'Torah in the Book of Jeremiah', pp. 382ff. In his commentary Hyatt
suggests that many have seen this passage as directed against Deuteronomy,
known in Jeremiah's day as 'the book of the law' (II Kings 22.8, 11; Deut.
30.10), '. . . and it is hard to imagine that any other book in Jeremiah's time
could have been the object of such confidence as is implied here. Yet Jeremiah
may well have been opposing the tendency to consider Deuteronomy and
other books as "scripture"; he was perhaps objecting to the very idea that
God's will can be crystallized in a book, especially if that book demands
sacrifice and glorifies the temple, and if those who use it become proud and
reject the living, oral word of the Lord through the prophet '(*IB* V, p. 882).
Leslie also interprets this passage in terms of the 'sharp antagonism between
priest and prophet,' *op. cit.*, p. 78.

[22] J. M. Myers, 'Scribe' in *IDB*; cf. also R. de Vaux, *Ancient Israel*, pp. 131f.

[23] Cf. Martin A. Klopfenstein, *Die Lüge nach dem Alten Testament* (Zürich:
Gotthelf-Verlag, 1964), pp. 133ff. In Klopfenstein's opinion this passage does
not set out a rigid opposition between 'word' and 'law', but is attacking an
institutionalization of both which fosters the feeling among the people that
they 'possess' Yahweh's law. 'Jeremiah has in mind a *tôrā* which no longer

2 They bend their tongue, their bow;
   falsehood and not truth has prevailed
                                in the land,
   for they go from wickedness to wickedness
     and they do not know me,
                                says Yahweh.
3 Let each man guard himself from his neighbour
     and do not trust every brother,
   for every brother is a deceiver
     and every neighbour goes about as a slanderer.
4 And each man cheats against his neighbour
     and they do not speak the truth.
   They taught their tongue to speak a lie;
     (in) wrong-doing they have wearied themselves.
5 Your dwelling is in the midst of deceit,
     with deceit they refused to know me.

It is noteworthy that it is 'sins of the tongue' which occupy the focal point of attention here. This is the kind of activity which takes place especially between those most closely related (brothers, friends; cf. the possible allusion to Jacob in vv. 3f., as well as the actions of Jeremiah's own family mirrored in 11.19; 12.6; 20.10). This is a kind of sin which is general to humanity (Rudolph cites examples of Egyptian complaints against the same type of activity) and is enhanced by a 'defective religiosity: because they do not know Yahweh, will have nothing to do with him, therefore all these sins which make the common life into a hell'.[24] This breakdown of the common life is also reflected in 9.7, which uses the image of the deceitful tongue which speaks 'peace' to the neighbour but secretly plots his ambush.

The point that a falsely-conceived notion of security, enhanced

---

provides the people with the occasion for a total return to Yahweh, but only with an opportunity of self-assertion against him. Instead of the *tôrā* being set up as a living claim of Yahweh over the people, the people now assert their rights over the *tôrā* and set over it the claim to be "wise" and to be in the right.'

[24] Rudolph, *op. cit.,* pp. 66f. Similarly Weiser, who says: 'the untruthfulness of the word is the characteristic of general decadence (cf. Ps. 12), and this has its ultimate basis in the absence of the knowledge of God' (*op. cit.,* p. 79). Dr G. W. Ahlström has suggested to me that v. 2 ('they go from wickedness to wickedness and do not know me') may represent the prophet's cutting comment upon a cult processional such as that which evoked Ps. 84 (cf. v. 8: 'They go from strength to strength; the God of gods will be seen in Zion!').

by the preaching of 'false' prophets, could have a disastrous effect on the nation has been made many times throughout this study. In this sense a pervasive religio-political *šeqer* could manifest itself as a decidedly negative and destructive force in the life of the nation. In 9.1–7 we face the same phenomenon on another level, as the power of *šeqer* undermines the reliability of personal intercommunication. The disease has extended to the very heart of the social order.

Any conclusions drawn from this study of the prophet's indictment of opponents and people must bear in mind the political situation which apparently forms the background of these oracles. We have noted that military imagery predominates, and that the coming political catastrophe is thought of as being imminent. That these events did not actually transpire until the time of Nebuchadnezzar need not concern us here. The important thing is that Jeremiah was convinced that the judgment of Yahweh was near and would certainly be carried out.

Although these early oracles are not so tightly organized and the polemic against falsehood not so systematically worked out as in those contexts we have discussed previously, one can still perceive in them the two familiar foci of our discussion. On the one hand, the people have come to conceive of their election as a guarantee of continued national security. Presumably, they did this not so much out of sheer stupidity, perversity, or blindness to the events of current history as out of a deep-seated misconception of the nature of their existence in relation to God. There is a genuine disagreement between these people and Jeremiah (cf. 5.12f.), just as there was later to be between that prophet and Hananiah (ch. 28).

On the other hand, if the people are seen to be rejecting what Jeremiah conceives to be the demands which Yahweh is making upon them (cf. 6.16–19; 8.7–9), this is not entirely their fault. Jeremiah also levels sharp attacks at their leaders, for these are the men who are primarily responsible for spreading a message of 'peace' where there is no peace (6.13ff.; 8.10ff.; 14.13–16). Believing what he did about the legitimate interpretation of the religious heritage and seeing the political danger which he was certain loomed just beyond the horizon, Jeremiah was forced to interpret the life of contemporary Judah in a way radically different from these prophets.

In the passages just studied it has become clear again that a prophet is made 'false' and known to be so on the basis of his message alone. And we see again that their *šeqer*-message is not only ineffective (i.e., unable to alter the course of events determined by Yahweh), but much worse: it is positively destructive, since by glossing over the real seriousness of the situation it prevents the only action on the part of the people which could possibly forestall the coming destructive judgment – repentance (cf. 7.3f.).

V

ŠEQER IN THE THEOLOGY OF JEREMIAH

THE main emphasis of this study has been on Jeremiah's use of the notion 'falsehood' to describe the sense of security which he felt was preventing the people of Judah from responding to Yahweh's call to repentance and the prophetic opponents, who were active purveyors of this message of 'peace'. For the sake of completeness, brief reference must be made to another area in which the prophet's notion of falsehood found expression, namely his polemic against idolatry.

I have elsewhere discussed this topic in detail, concentrating my attention on an analysis of the structure and content of Jeremiah 10.1–16 viewed in the context of the shape of the polemic against idolatry found in the remainder of the book.[1] It is unnecessary to repeat the details of that study here, although some of its general conclusions should be cited as relevant to the present investigation. It was argued that Jer. 10.1–16 displayed a definite structural pattern, in which hymn-like praises addressed to or spoken about Yahweh alternate with statements critical of idols. The function of this pattern is to press home the contrast between Yahweh and the gods whose symbols the idols are. This scheme was seen to recur in the utterances of Jeremiah in passages like 2.8–13, 26–28; 3.1–5, 23; 5.20–25; 14.22; and 16.19–20. The question of why the prophet felt moved to brand these gods and their cultic practices 'false' (3.23; 10.14; 16.19) seems best answered in terms of his perception of their basic ineffectiveness.

It is interesting that the prophet compares Yahweh with the gods in terms of their own special functions, and not by playing off his capability of historical action against their bondage to

---

[1] 'The Falsehood of Idolatry: An Interpretation of Jer. x. 1–16', *JTS*, NS 16 (1965), pp. 1–12. In my view the methodological implications of this study are inseparable from and at least as important as the conclusions it reached about the specific interpretation of Jer. 10.1–16.

nature, as if the latter in itself made them inferior. In the broader sense it is true that Jeremiah conceived of Yahweh as pre-eminently a God of history, yet in terms of this one concrete aspect of his polemic the prophet is conceiving of him as the creator and ruler of nature. By comparison with him the gods of the nations are 'vain' (*hebhel*), powerless even to accomplish those functions for which they are specialists. Consequently, the cultus connected with such gods is also ineffective. Only in Yahweh is the 'salvation' of Israel to be found (3.23).[2]

Our task is now to attempt to understand the meaning and function of the term *šeqer* in the theological vocabulary of the prophet Jeremiah. But in order to put his use of the term in a proper perspective, some remarks are in order about its use outside the book of Jeremiah.[3] While the noun *šeqer* is found 36 times in Jeremiah, it also occurs frequently in the Pentateuch, Psalms, and Proverbs, and it will be convenient to limit the following brief remarks to those three blocks of material.[4]

Seven of the eight occurrences of *šeqer* in the Pentateuch are in what we might call a 'legal' context. That is to say, the topic under discussion in each of them is false witness, swearing falsely, or

---

[2] Because of his conviction that the term *šeqer* refers basically to a breach of relationship, often of the covenant relationship which exists between the people and Yahweh, Martin A. Klopfenstein argues that the intention of Jer. 3.23 is not to say that idol worship *is* *šeqer*, but that it *leads to šeqer* (i.e., breach of the covenant). Only in passages like Jer. 16.19; 10.14, and Isa. 44.20 does *šeqer* cease to describe personal behaviour and come to refer to the 'ineffectiveness' of the idols themselves. The latter constitutes a decided 'fading' of the original connotation. See *Die Lüge nach dem Alten Testament*, pp. 83ff. At least in the case of Jeremiah, one wonders if such a distinction is necessary. In his polemic the ineffectiveness of the people's false sense of security for coping with the contemporary political situation seems functionally equivalent to that ascribed to the gods: neither were capable of altering the course of events which Yahweh has willed.

[3] While *šeqer* is but one of the Hebrew roots which convey the basic notion of 'falsehood', it is the only one that has been systematically used by Jeremiah in his prophetic utterances. Klopfenstein has done an exhaustive study of all the roots, and his conclusions about the sphere in which each was originally at home are of interest: *šqr* is basically a term from the sphere of treaty law, *khš* from that of criminal law, *šaw'* from that of primitive magic, and *kzb* from daily life. *Op. cit.*, pp. 321f.

[4] The verb is infrequent in the Old Testament. Klopfenstein maintains that its basic meaning relates to the breaking of an agreement rather than to some kind of 'lying' speech (Gen. 21.23; Pss. 89.34; 44.18), and cites eighth-century Aramaic treaties of state in which the root *šqr* functions as a technical term for the breaking of a treaty' (*op. cit.*, pp. 8ff.).

speaking falsely, and all of these are viewed as a perversion of justice. Probably the most familiar example of this usage comes from the Decalogue itself: 'You shall not bear false witness (*'ed šāqer*) against your neighbour' (Ex. 20.16; cf. 23.7; Lev. 5.22, 24; 19.12; Deut. 19.18, where the term occurs twice). The basic meaning here is non-correspondence to 'fact'. What the 'false witness' does is accuse someone of doing a thing which he in fact did not do (cf. Deut. 19.15–19). He tells a 'lie' in our everyday sense of that term. An actual example of this kind of lying is found in II Kings 9.12. After being privately anointed by Elisha, Jehu emerges into the presence of his servants but seeks to deceive them by implying that nothing took place between the prophet and himself. In the face of this rather suspicious assertion the men reply, 'It is a lie! Tell us now (what really happened)!'

The one exception to this 'legal' usage of the term is Ex. 5.9, which is part of the narrative describing Pharaoh's reaction to Moses' initial demand that the people of Israel be allowed to make a pilgrimage into the wilderness to worship Yahweh. Angered by this request, he ordered the foremen to withhold straw from the captive labourers but not to reduce the number of bricks required of them, so that they would have no time or inclination to 'regard lying words'. That is, Pharaoh was in effect saying the same thing about Yahweh's promise of deliverance (Ex. 3.7–10; 5.1–3) that we found Jeremiah saying about the gods, viz. he is ineffective, unable to carry out the promise made.

The term *šeqer* occurs 22 times in the Psalter in a total of 14 psalms: 7,27, 31, 33, 35, 38, 52, 63, 69, 101, 109, 119 (eight times), 120, 144 (twice). According to Gunke's classification, most of these are to be viewed as individual laments (the exceptions are: 27.1–6, a song of trust; 33, a choir-hymn; 101, an enthronement proclamation: 144, a royal lament; and 119, an alphabetical psalm of mixed form).[5]

Beginning with those *šeqer*-psalms which may be classified as laments (of whatever sort), we may note that almost without exception the term *šeqer* is used as descriptive of the actions of the enemies. As one would expect, it occurs for the most part in two

---

[5] H. Gunkel and J. Begrich, *Einleitung in die Psalmen* (Göttingen: Vandenhoeck und Ruprecht, 1929 and 1933). H.-J. Kraus, *Psalmen,* arrives at substantially the same classification.

elements of these psalms: the lament[6] and the prayer.[7] 27.12 is especially instructive, for the enemies are here described as 'false witnesses' (*ʿēdhê šeqer*), and this appears to be the burden of their offence against the suppliant. Throughout these psalms, in fact, the plotting of the enemies is predominantly oral in nature (cf. 31.19; 35.1, 11, 20f., 25; 52.4–6; 120.2; etc.). Thus two-thirds of the occurrences of *šeqer* in the Psalter come in laments, in which the term performs the function of referring to the enemies' actions. This action may be generally characterized as the bearing of false witness and involvement in plots against the suppliant. The major emphasis, then, is on the use of the term 'lie' in the sense of untruth or non-correspondence to fact. The connotation of the term in these psalms is heavily legal, as it is also in several psalms outside the lament group.[8] In only two passages (33.17; 119.118, where the connotation 'ineffectiveness' seems to be called for) do we find clear indications that something other than a legal context is to be thought of where the term occurs.

Our understanding of these occurrences of *šeqer* will depend somewhat on how we conceive of the individual psalms of lamentation. For Gunkel this group formed the backbone of the Psalter, and represented the prayers of real, private individuals.[9] S. Mowinckel, on the other hand, suggests that these are in fact royal psalms, or national laments in the 'I-form'.[10] H. Birkeland concurs in this judgment, arguing that the enemies of the individuals here represented are identical with those of the nation.[11] He cites, for example, the fact that numerous psalms contain war imagery and speak of 'falsity' or 'false witness' (27, 31, 35, 69, etc.), and refers to the Amarna letters as providing us with the most

[6] 27.12; 52.5; 63.12; 69.5; 109.2. In 7.15 the term appears in a narrative section, which is perhaps most akin to the lament.

[7] 31.19; 35.19; 120.2; 144.8, 11.

[8] Ps. 101 is in effect the king's promise (doubtless uttered in connection with his enthronement) to maintain justice in the land, so the reference to 'those who utter lies' (*dôbhrê šeqārîm*, v. 7) probably refers to persons who in more strictly legal terminology would be designated *ʿēdhê šeqer*. In several passages in Ps. 119 walking in *šeqer* (etc.) is specifically rejected in favour of Yahweh's *tôrāh* (vv. 29, 163) or *piqqûdhîm* (vv. 104, 128). The other occurrences of *šeqer* in this psalm are within lament contexts (vv. 69, 78, 86).

[9] *Op. cit.*, paragraphs 3, 4, 5, 30.

[10] *The Psalms in Israel's Worship.*

[11] *The Evildoers in the Book of Psalms* (Oslo: Dybwad, 1955), p. 9. This book is a restatement of the argument of his earlier work, *Die Feinde des Individuums in der Israelitische Psalmenliteratur* (Oslo: Grondahl, 1933).

plausible background for understanding this phenomenon: Israel is under foreign domination, and 'false witnesses' appear accusing the vassal king before his overlord. Falsity thus has a legal connotation (untrue accusation) and belongs 'to the patternized qualities of the enemies'.[12]

It would thus seem that the term *šeqer* in the psalms retains the same basic connotation which we found it representing in the legal material of the Pentateuch, centring on the notion of 'lie' as 'non-correspondence to fact'.[13]

Finally, some comments are in order regarding the 20 occurrences of the noun in Proverbs. It is widely recognized that this book is not a literary unity, but is rather 'the outcome of a process of thought and work that continued for centuries, and in which writing was a by-product of oral teaching'.[14] Several collections (often displaying independent headings; cf. 10.1; 25.1) are evident within the book, the oldest of which is probably the 'Proverbs of Solomon' (10.1–22.16),[15] although the process of development of even this section may have extended into the exilic period or beyond.[16] The bulk of the occurrences of *šeqer* (13) are within this section of the book.

Again, it is the 'legal' sense of the term which predominates. In several instances the condemnation of 'false witness' is explicit, as, for example, the couplet:

> He who speaks the truth gives honest evidence,
> but a false witness utters deceit (12.17).[17]

Other couplets characterize the lips or tongue which conceal the true feelings, intent, or actions of their owners as *šeqer*,[18] and the

---

[12] *Evildoers . . .*, p. 32.

[13] Klopfenstein agrees that the use of *šeqer* in the Psalms corresponds to that of the passages which speak of false testimony and oaths. He takes pains to point out that whoever is guilty of such perjury is in breach of the covenant with Yahweh (*op. cit.*, pp. 40f., 78f.).

[14] J. Coert Rylaarsdam, *Proverbs, Ecclesiastes, Song of Solomon* (Richmond: John Knox Press; London: SCM Press, 1964), p. 9.

[15] Cf. J. Coert Rylaarsdam, 'The Proverbs', *Peake's Commentary*, ed. M. Black and H. H. Rowley (2nd ed. rev.; London: Thomas Nelson, 1962).

[16] Cf. O. Eissfeldt, *The Old Testament: An Introduction*, trans. P. R. Ackroyd (Oxford: Blackwell, and New York: Harper and Row, 1965), pp. 473f.; R. B. Y. Scott, *Proverbs, Ecclesiastes* (The Anchor Bible, Garden City: Doubleday, 1965), pp. 17f.

[17] Cf. also 6.19; 14.5; 19.5, 9; 25.18.

[18] 6.17; 10.18; 12.19; 26.28.

general notion is that only the unrighteous or wicked man engages in such activity (described in 12.22 as 'an abomination to Yahweh').[19] Several times the term is used in general axioms.[20] This concrete and practical use of the term is what one would expect in the earliest Israelite collection of wisdom material, for the purpose of this movement itself 'was initially a very practical one: to educate the nobility for cultural and political leadership'.[21]

One additional comment can be made. G. von Rad has argued that from the beginning Israel's empirical wisdom was involved in an attempt to perceive the truth about human existence, to discern the 'kindly' order which lay 'at the bottom of things'. It was, therefore, 'an attempt to safeguard life and to master it on the broad basis of experience'.[22] If such a description is accurate, then one might say that the type of activity referred to by the term *šeqer* represents not so much a simply neutral entity in the scheme of things as an actual threat to the continued harmonious existence of this 'kindly' order of life.

To sum up, in the blocks of Old Testament material just discussed the legal usage of the term *šeqer* predominates, although some extension of that meaning is already present in such passages as Ex. 5.9 and Pss. 33.17; 119.118.

We might expect that in the process of employing the noun *šeqer* as one of the important concepts in his theological vocabulary, Jeremiah would not lose sight of the predominant legal sense in which the term was usually employed, but would rather build upon and enlarge it. This is in fact the case, and there are several occasions in the later narrative chapters of the book in which the term *šeqer* is employed in the common, everyday sense of our word 'lie'. Once, during a temporary lifting of the siege of Jerusalem, the prophet attempted to leave the city on family business. When stopped at the gate by a sentry, who accused him of wanting to desert to the Chaldeans, he replied, 'It is a lie! I am not deserting to the Chaldeans' (*wayyō'mer jirmᵉyāhû šeqer 'ênennî nōphēl 'al-hakkasdîm*, 37.14; cf. 40.16 and 43.2).

---

[19] 11.18; 13.5; 17.4; 20.17; 21.6.

[20] 29.12 ('If a ruler listens to *šeqer* / all his officials will be wicked'), 31.30 ('Charm is *šeqer* and beauty *hebhel* / but a woman who fears Yahweh is to be praised'); also 17.7 and 25.14.

[21] Rylaarsdam, *Proverbs . . .*, p. 9.

[22] *Theology* I, pp. 418–21, 428, 432.

Yet we have seen that for the most part Jeremiah's own view of those things which could be characterized as *šeqer* (the misconception of the nature of the security afforded by Yahweh's election of the nation, the words of his prophetic opponents, confidence in other gods) was that they were ineffective, powerless to change the real situation confronting the people. They served only to gloss over the trouble spots and prevent any amelioration of the situation, for they counselled a course of action diametrically opposed to that which would have been necessary to avoid the coming destruction of the city, temple, and land. To use a concrete example, they encouraged the people to think that Nebuchadnezzar's rule of Palestine would be of short duration, and the outcome of this encouragement was revolt and destruction rather than the continued existence of the nation in its land which might have followed acknowledging the Babylonian king's presence as an act of punishment ordained by Yahweh (ch. 27).

Simply to cite such an example is to emphasize the fact that any discussion of the activity of either Jeremiah or his opponents has to make sense within the context of the concrete historical situation of the last days of the Judean kingdom. We have even to see these prophets as belonging to opposing political parties or persuasions: Jeremiah and some of the princes (notably the family of Shaphan) were pro-Babylonian in their sentiments, while king Jehoiakim, a large number of princes, and (presumably) prophets like Hananiah maintained a pro-Egyptian stance.

Now it was the job of a prophet to interpret current events on the basis of a certain set of theological insights or assumptions, and we need to remember that Jeremiah and the other classical prophets were not the only ones engaged in this interpretative activity. His opponents also had their views concerning the meaning and outcome of the events of their day, and these were often quite different from the notions espoused by Jeremiah (e.g., the conflict over the length of the exile). Both were performing the same function, and the crucial questions are why they differed and the basis upon which one is able to decide between the two.

Put in this way, the problem is seen as one which directly affects only Jeremiah's contemporaries. From the standpoint of a later day it is a simple matter to vindicate Jeremiah, for the judgment of which he spoke came to pass with striking finality in the second conquest of Jerusalem. But for individuals who found themselves standing in the actual complicated historical situation of, say, Judah between the two deportations, the matter would not have been so simple. Confronted by men of such diverse opinions as Hananiah and Jeremiah, they would have found themselves faced with the necessity of making an important religious and political choice. This was not merely a choice between men, but a choice between alternative courses of action in pursuit of the goal of national security and survival. Nor could the decision be put off. Events were rolling towards a climax, and if the decision was to have any effect upon their outcome, it would have to be reached before the climax arrived. In a deeper sense, the fall of Jerusalem in 586 was less a vindication of Jeremiah than a clear indication of his failure to get his message across persuasively enough for the people to take the proper steps to avert the disaster.

The Hananiah episode makes it abundantly clear that the actual auditors of the prophet's message did not have available to them any 'objective' criterion like that of the 'fulfilment of prophecy' in terms of which they could judge between rival claims. Whatever validity is to be attributed to the words which Jeremiah delivered to his people during the course of four decades resides less in any fulfilment which they might subsequently have attained than in the assumption on which they were based, namely, that Yahweh was in control of the events of history and in the exercise of this control was free to confront his people in new and sometimes destructive ways in any period of their existence.

Of course, to put the matter this way is simply to restate, and not solve, the problem. Jeremiah's opponents also knew that Yahweh was in control of history. This is clearly the case with Hananiah, who expects that 'within two years' Yahweh will bring the captives and temple vessels back from Babylon to Jerusalem (28.2–4). In Hananiah and Jeremiah, then, we are confronted by two differing interpretations of the way in which Yahweh was acting in current history.

It ought to be fairly clear that in matters of this sort definite proof is seldom if ever available. Even if the opponents had pointed explicitly to the optimistic traditions of the great covenants, this 'evidence' would have been unconvincing to Jeremiah. Likewise, Jeremiah's designation of their activity as *šeqer* was merely his own assessment of the situation. Both interpretations are ultimately based upon an evaluation of current events in the light of certain theological traditions. And how can we distinguish between the two modes of appropriating the traditions of the past? In attempting to answer this question it seems useful to me to suggest that Jeremiah's interpretations rest upon an affirmation of Yahweh's radical freedom to deal with his people in ways appropriate to their present situation, while those of his opponents are characterized by a tendency to accept the traditional patterns of the faith as normative for all of Yahweh's action, past and future. Both are attempts to remain faithful to the valued traditions of the past, yet in the conflict between them we have a striking example of the age-old tension between more or less rigid institutional expressions of the 'faith' and continuing attempts dynamically to appropriate this faith in terms relevant to the complexities of a contemporary historical situation.

It is important that we do not make the mistake of viewing these two tendencies as mutually exclusive. It would be more accurate to see them as opposing points on a continuum. Both Jeremiah and his opponents are to be placed at appropriate spots on a relative scale between them. Neither, for example, thought of Yahweh as absolutely free with regard to his dealings with Judah. It was inconceivable to Hananiah that Yahweh would ever completely abandon the nation, and so for him the capitulation of 597 must have seemed like punishment enough against the people. Surely Yahweh would now restore their fortunes. One could thus with good conscience even counsel revolt against Nebuchadnezzar, feeling no incongruity between this action and Yahweh's will. Jeremiah, as we know, felt differently. Yet although it was within his capabilities to see and understand a complete destruction of the nation at Yahweh's hands, he could not conceive of this as being the last word in the matter. And it is precisely in his envisioning of a 'new covenant' between Yahweh and his people (31.31–34) that his own deep-rooted sympathies with his opponents come clearly to light (cf. 28.6). The difference between him and his opponents is one of degree, not kind.

The political and social situation of the mid-twentieth century has a way of presenting itself to us as a highly (often a bewilderingly) complex set of phenomena. I would suspect that the people of ancient Israel, especially those living in times of major crisis, had a similar feeling about the political and religious forces at work in their day. Not all situations were the same, nor would there necessarily be agreement among interpreters of a single situation. As a case in point, the contrast between the views of two great prophets, Isaiah and Jeremiah, with regard to the fate of Zion shows clearly that a prophet could view a coming period of disaster in any one of several ways. Isaiah said that Zion would be saved,[23] while Jeremiah insisted that it would perish. What does this difference of opinion reflect?

It is improbable that the difference resides simply in the fact that, after a close political analysis, Isaiah found the position of the nation in his day to be less vulnerable than Jeremiah did in his. It is questionable to assume that, from a realistic point of view, military defeat looked any less imminent to Isaiah than it did to Jeremiah. For Isaiah's contemporary, Micah, it seemed clear that the city would fall (3.12), and the seriousness of the situation is further demonstrated by Sennacherib's own account of the Palestinian campaign in which he tells how he captured forty-six Judean cities and made Hezekiah himself 'a prisoner in Jerusalem, his royal residence, like a bird in a cage'.[24]

However, the religious situation in Judah does seem to have looked better to Isaiah than to Jeremiah. For the former, although the people had been sinful and must be punished, a remnant would return and be established in the land (cf. 7.3; 4.2ff.; 10.20–22; 11.10–16; 28.5f.; 37.32). Jeremiah, however, had arrived at a new estimate of the situation of the people, one which saw them incapable of any change which would be sufficient to preserve the old means of relationship to Yahweh (2.20–22; 13.22f.).[25]

It is interesting to note that from the earliest days of his ministry Jeremiah announced the coming of destruction from the North. We have seen that this theme is strong in chs. 4–6 and 8–9. Only at a later date (after the battle of Carchemish) is this foe explicitly identified with the Babylonians (25.9). It would therefore appear that the prophet was announcing punishment against a sinful people even before the concrete political threat of such punishment was imminent. As a matter of fact, the historical

---

[23] See the passages cited above, p. 40, n.30.

[24] *ANET*, p. 288.

[25] While this description of Isaiah's attitude toward Zion seems essentially correct, passages like 29.2, 4 reveal a certain 'theological ambivalence' in his view concerning Yahweh's judgment against the people. Cf. von Rad, *Theology* II, pp. 164ff., 174f., and B. S. Childs, *Isaiah and the Assyrian Crisis* (SBT, Second Series, 3, 1967), pp. 20–68.

situation at the time of these oracles must have made the prophet's message seem quite strange. It seems probable that Palestine was not threatened by an invasion of Scythians during this period. Furthermore, Judah under Josiah was again beginning to assert herself politically by taking advantage of the increasing weakness of the Assyrian empire to recoup for herself portions of the Davidic kingdom which she had not controlled for centuries. Thus Jeremiah was predicting doom for the people when little was yet in sight, another indication that his message must be seen as a complicated mixture of theological assumptions and political astuteness.[26]

[26] These statements presuppose a date of 627/26 for the prophet's call, based on the evidence of 1.1f. and 25.3. This traditional date has, however, been challenged, in recent times most persistently by H. P. Hyatt, who originally argued that the prophet's call should be dated in the period 614–612 but later came to view 609 as a preferable date. Cf. 'The Peril from the North in Jeremiah', *JBL* 59 (1940), pp. 499–513; 'Jeremiah and Deuteronomy', *JNES* 1 (1942), pp. 156–73; 'Jeremiah: Introduction and Exegesis', *IB* V (1956); and 'The Beginning of Jeremiah's Prophecy', *ZAW* 78 (1966), pp. 204–14. In the latter article he is debating C. F. Whitley's view that the call occurred in 605; cf. Whitley's 'The Date of Jeremiah's Call', *VT* 14 (1964), pp. 467–83, and his rejoinder to Hyatt, 'Carchemish and Jeremiah', *ZAW* 80 (1968), pp. 38–49. Although this is not the place for a detailed critique of such arguments, some brief objections to Hyatt's reconstruction seem warranted. First of all, it is worth noting that this reconstruction flies in the face of the only explicit evidence we have regarding the date of the prophet's call (1.2; 25.3). Secondly, although he is historically correct in pointing to the improbability of a Scythian invasion of Palestine, Hyatt is guilty of making certain rather problematic assumptions about the whole notion of an enemy from the North. He assumes, for instance, that this foe must be actually named and concretely real, but in his treatment of the early oracles Rudolph has convincingly pointed out that no concrete designation of an enemy completely corresponds to the prophet's description and that, furthermore, the focus of attention is rather upon Yahweh's punishment of a sinful people and not on the identification and description of the foe. That the early oracles eventually find their fulfilment (at least as far as the prophet himself is concerned) in the rise to power of the Neo-Babylonian state, cannot be denied (Cf. 25.9, and see *op. cit.,* pp. 47–49. Cf. also A. S. Kapelrud's treatment of 'the northerner' in *Joel Studies,* Uppsala: Almquist and Wiksells, 1948, pp. 93–108.) Thirdly, both Hyatt and Whitley seem to be motivated by the assumption that it is necessary to 'save' a great prophet like Jeremiah from the embarrassment and discredit involved in being wrong about the imminence of the coming destruction. Thus Hyatt: 'This date removes the difficulty of supposing that Jeremiah once supported the Deuteronomic reforms and later turned against them; and also of supposing that the prophet was discredited by prediction of a peril from the north which did not materialize and then went into retirement in disgrace, only to emerge after Josiah's death' (1940, p. 513). And Whitley: 'To suppose that Jeremiah was mistaken in his first utterances and was compelled to modify them in accordance with later

Here it may be relevant to recall that form criticism of the prophetic oracle has taught us that the normal utterance of a prophet consisted of two parts: an exhortation or diatribe, followed by a word from Yahweh. The latter element is normally distinguished from the former by the intervening 'messenger formula', 'Thus says Yahweh. . . .' It is commonly thought that the diatribe (*'Begründung'*) is the prophet's own analysis of the situation into which he speaks his message, while the word itself (*'Gerichts-ankündigung'*) constitutes the message received from Yahweh.[27] This means that the individual prophet possessed a large degree of freedom in developing an analysis of the situation which he could preface to Yahweh's word, as well as in choosing an appropriate form in which to express this analysis and even an appropriate audience to hear it.[28] Perhaps this is why Jeremiah was briefly stumped by Hananiah's announcement of imminent restoration. It may be that he had to retire precisely to rethink this analysis of the political situation and the condition of the people. But his assumptions about Yahweh's freedom and the people's condition remained constant, and thus the result of his re-evaluation was the same as his original message.

It is evident that there was more than one view of Yahweh's activity current in Jeremiah's day. The prophet himself pictured him as acting through Nebuchadnezzar in judgment upon a sinful people. Hananiah, on the other hand, saw him as about to initiate

---

developments likewise overlooks the efficacy of the divine word' (1968, p. 48). Both seem to overlook the fact that the prophet himself felt discredited during much of the early part of his career (cf. 20.7f.). Unlike them, I do not find the possibility that Jeremiah gradually sharpened his perception of the 'foe from the North' to be beyond comprehension: cf. my 'King Nebuchadnezzar in the Jeremiah Tradition', *CBQ* 30 (1968), pp. 39–48. I do not want to assert that the problem of the date of Jeremiah's call and related matters (such as the supposed absence of oracles datable in Josiah's reign and his connection, or lack of it, with the Deuteronomic reform) are simply solved, but only that to this point I remain unconvinced by evidence cited against the traditional date. On the other hand, two articles may be mentioned as having implications which seem to strengthen the position of supporters of the traditional date: R. Davidson, 'Orthodoxy and the Prophetic Word', *VT* 14 (1964), pp. 407–16, and W. Johnstone, 'The Setting of Jeremiah's Prophetic Activity', *Trans-actions of the Glasgow University Oriental Society* 21 (1965–66), pp. 47–55.

[27] G. von Rad, *Theology* II, pp. 36–39; C. Westermann, *Basic Forms of Prophetic Speech*, trans. H. C. White (Philadelphia: Westminster, 1967), pp. 169ff.

[28] G. von Rad, *Theology* II, pp. 70ff.

on behalf of his people a great act of restoration. But there were
others whose views were different again:

> He will do nothing;
>   no evil will come upon us,
>   nor will we see sword and famine.
> The prophets will become wind,
>   the word is not in them. (Jer. 5.12f.)
> Yahweh will not do good,
>   nor will he do evil. (Zeph. 1.12)

Von Rad has commented that these statements are not those of
'atheists', but rather of men who 'no longer reckoned with divine
action in the present day'. The present political crisis left the
'question of Yahweh's relationship to his people completely
uncertain'. His 'purpose' could no longer be discerned behind the
events of history.[29]

Why was this so? Presumably, part of the reason would be that
the Yahweh faith was simply not shared by all the people of
Judah in Jeremiah's day or in any other. We too often forget that
the Old Testament is the product of a religious movement, whose
assumptions it reflects and defends. It is difficult to envision the
time when the entire Israelite community actively embraced its
brand of religious 'orthodoxy' (exclusive worship of Yahweh,
etc.).[30] Yet it is evident that even many 'religious' people of
Jeremiah's day had adopted a rather static view of Yahweh and his
ability and inclination to act in their history. That is to say, their
theological outlook was characterized by a tendency which
threatens all institutions, a tendency to absolutize certain portions
of their heritage. They formed guidelines within which Yahweh
was thought to act. In this they were probably no different from
their fathers before them, though such a recognition could not
have justified in Jeremiah's eyes a course of action which he
viewed as particularly disastrous.[31]

---

[29] *Ibid.*, II, p. 263.

[30] Cf. *ibid.*, II, 341, and especially Th. G. Vriezen, *An Outline of Old
Testament Theology*, ch. 2, where a distinction is made between three separate
but interrelated phenomena; 'the ancient oriental religious world, the religion
of Israel, and the Old Testament' (p. 14).

[31] Klopfenstein makes a similar point, noting that when *šeqer* is used to
describe the utterances of the prophetic opponents it points to the fact that
they do not give sufficient room to the 'freedom of divine action,' (*op. cit.*,
p. 119).

This study began with an examination of Jeremiah's Temple Sermon, which revealed the promise of the covenant (or election) traditions as the source of the people's false feeling of security. More sharply than many of his contemporaries, the prophet saw that the maintenance of the relationship to Yahweh celebrated in those traditions depended upon the people's fulfilling of two broad conditions: the preserving of a just social order and of a cult dedicated to Yahweh alone. Although they were aware of these conditions, their inclination to centre their thought on the positive side of the traditions dulled their sensitivity to their misdeeds in the social and religious spheres and the threat of the political situation.

The discussion of Jeremiah's encounters with the prophetic opponents has indicated how these men took up this misconception and fostered it. For it has been seen again and again that what made these prophets 'false' was the content of the message which they proclaimed: 'peace'. As Jeremiah interpreted the situation, they were making this proclamation without sufficient regard for either the condition of the people or the current political threat.

One of the organizing insights in von Rad's treatment of Old Testament theology is that with the advent of prophecy something radically new was being said to the Israelite people about their relationship with Yahweh:

However overpoweringly diverse (the prophetic movement) may be, it nevertheless has its starting point in the conviction that Israel's previous history with Yahweh has come to an end, and that he will start something new with her. The prophets seek to convince their contemporaries that for them the hitherto existing saving ordinances have lost their worth, and that, if Israel is to be saved, she must move in faith into a new saving activity of Yahweh, one which is only to come in the future. But this conviction of theirs, that what has existed till now is broken off, places them basically outside the saving history as it had been understood up to then by Israel. The prophets' message had its centre and its bewildering dynamic effect in the fact that it smashed in pieces Israel's existence with God up to the present, and rang up the curtain of history for a new action on his part with her.[32]

The prophetic message was based upon a continuing dynamic perception of the ways in which Yahweh was presently acting with his people. Because he viewed reality in this way, Jeremiah

[32] *Theology* I, p. 128.

could announce the destruction of the nation and affirm the continuing lordship of Nebuchadnezzar over the nations. He could, in other words, see the sure result of the habitual course of religious, social, and political action of the people and their leaders. But because of his stronger orientation to the essentially positive aspects of the tradition, a prophet such as Hananiah was not so radically free in his conception of Yahweh's activity. The break between him and Judah was seen to be less complete, and its grounds less serious. Punishment had already come. Could restoration be far behind? To put it another way, the flexibility of his theological outlook allowed Jeremiah to be much more open to the fact of Babylon's overwhelming political power and appreciative of the inevitable consequences of that fact for Judah's national existence. By contrast the relative rigidity of Hananiah's theology enabled him more easily to ignore (or at least take a less realistic attitude towards) the press of historical events.[33]

There is, we discover, no easy answer to the listener's dilemma. There is no simple formula by which a contemporary could determine whether Jeremiah or his opponents were 'false'. We do not know how many threw in their lot with Jeremiah, although the fact that Judah rose in a final, disastrous revolt against Nebuchadnezzar at least implies that many of the influential persons of the government did not. Some of the princes did support him, however (cf. 26.24; 36.9–26), notably the members of the house of Shaphan, and the fact that he received such strong support from the latter family may yield an important clue with regard to the 'listener's dilemma'. Shaphan ben Azaliah was a high official under Josiah (*sōphēr*, II Kings 22.3) and was from the beginning in on the discovery of the law-book and the reform of the cultus. He and the members of his family would thus be especially sensitive to both aspects of the election traditions: promise and obligation. In this respect it is interesting to contrast the reaction of Josiah (and presumably Shaphan) to the finding of the law-book (II Kings 22.11, 19) and that of Micaiah and Gemariah (along with some other princes) to the reading of Baruch's roll (Jer. 36.16, 25) with the reaction of Jehoiakim and his supporters to that roll (Jer. 36.22–24). Jeremiah's message would for the most part have been

[33] For a discussion of Jeremiah's response to the collapse of Judah cf. P. R. Ackroyd, *Exile and Restoration* (London: SCM Press, and Philadelphia: Westminster, 1968), pp. 50–61.

understood and accepted only by those who had (or in whom could be aroused) some sensitivity to the full range and complexity of the nation's theological heritage. Both understanding and acceptance would certainly be hindered if the listener were a staunch member of the pro-Egyptian camp.

The message of Jeremiah is dominated by the notion of 'falsehood'. It could have been otherwise. The prophet might conceivably have emphasized a number of other concepts and still got his message across. Is it possible to decide why the term *šeqer* fits his needs so well? The key to this question would seem to reside in an observation that we have made several times in passing: the term *šeqer* implies the operation of a destructive power, and is thus peculiarly applicable to the social, political, and religious situation in which the prophet worked.[34] J. Pedersen's views on the Israelite conception of society are very suggestive in this regard.

For a man to be isolated from his fellows was, in the Old Testament view of things, an unnatural condition. Man exists in a community, which is (or ought to be) characterized by a common will and a common sense of responsibility. At its base, this community rests upon a covenant which manifests itself in the 'peace' or 'wholeness' (*šalôm*) of mutual confidence between human beings.[35] The reality 'covenant' is thus conceived in a very broad sense:

All life is common life, and so peace and covenant are really denominations of life itself. One is born of a covenant and into a covenant, and wherever one moves in life, one makes a covenant or acts on the basis of the already existing covenant. If everything that comes under the term of covenant were dissolved, existence would fall to pieces, because no soul can live an isolated life . . . it is in direct conflict with its essence to be something apart.[36]

Such important qualities of existence as justice and truth (*'emeth*) presuppose a covenant relationship. The individual can live and act only in unity with others. He is but a link in a larger totality which 'creates a centre of will. To be just and true means to subject the whole contents of one's soul to this centre of will,

---

[34] On numerous occasions Klopfenstein makes reference to the destructive power of *šeqer* within the community. See, for example, pp. 23, 32, 94, 98f., 106, 109f., 129, 131, 161ff.

[35] J. Pedersen, *Israel: Its Life and Culture* I-II, pp. 263ff.

[36] *Ibid.*, p. 308.

to identify one's will with that of the totality'. Man is thus an organic part of a whole system of expectations. And because this is so, justice is for him both 'a privilege and a claim'. He is bound to respond to both its benefits and its requirements.[37]

Šeqer enters this discussion as the correlative of *'emeth*. As Pedersen describes it, a sinful act is one which is split off from the 'firm centre of action' provided by a covenant. 'Falsehood' is characteristic of the split soul of the man who acts in this way. By virtue of its grounding in the common will and responsibility of the community, truth has the strength to maintain itself. But falsehood is without basis in this totality. It is 'hollow and rootless'. Since 'it is not filled with the substance of a soul', it is 'inefficient (and) powerless' (cf. Ps. 33.17). Sin and falsehood act outside the laws of the covenant which upholds life.[38]

In applying these insights to the material of the present study, we must begin with the recognition that both Jeremiah and his opponents were members of the same broad social, religious, and political community, and both were ultimately interested in the welfare of that group. Certainly Jeremiah was concerned in the years after 597 to prevent actions on the part of the people which would lead to further destruction (cf. 28.6). In this sense he too was a prophet of peace. And yet the perceptions which each had of the prevailing situation of the nation were quite different. For the opponents it seemed beyond question that at its core the covenant basis of the community remained healthy. Because of this they could cry out to the people in Yahweh's name, 'You will not see the sword, and you will not have famine, for you will have *šalôm 'emeth* in this place' (14.13).

Jeremiah could label this affirmation *šeqer* (14.14) because of his different reading of the total situation. Over and over again in his utterances we are aware that he looks upon the community not as a healthy whole, but as tragically broken. The *'emeth*, *mišpāṭ*, and *ṣedaqâ* characteristic of a healthy community were gone, and must be asserted again by a repentant people who actively return to Yahweh (4.1f.). The situation which he saw was characterized by a breakdown in the harmony between man and man (9.1–7; *šeqer* is

---

[37] *Ibid.*, pp. 340–42.

[38] *Ibid.*, pp. 411–15. Klopfenstein concludes his study with the remark that we can summarize the Old Testament's basic evaluation of falsehood in the simple assertion: 'Falsehood is hostile to the community' (*op. cit.*, p. 353).

displacing *'emeth*, v. 4) and man and Yahweh, and an actual heightening of the causes of this breakdown by the national leaders. Wholeness was gone, and could be restored only by a future turning of God towards his people (32.36–41; 33.1–9).

Because of its brokenness, the national life can be characterized by the term *šeqer*. In this kind of context that term transcends the everyday notion of prevarication and becomes descriptive of an insidious destructive force at work among the people. This is true first of all because *šeqer* points us to the empty centre of the communal life. The inner harmony was gone, and in its place was a hollowness which prepared the way for collapse. Harmony could only be brought back by a radical change on the part of the people: 'Amend your ways and your doings, and I will let you dwell in this place. . .' (7.3). Had the people responded to this call to repentance they might have regained a common centre of will and been again on the road to communal health and wholeness. But anything less than this radical response would be like attempting to cure a cancer with cold cream.

But beyond this pointing to the void at the centre of life, the people's *šeqer* emerged as a force actively working against any amelioration of the present situation. It was able to do this by obscuring the real nature and seriousness of the illness that plagued the communal life. The lopsided confidence in Yahweh's relationship to the nation and the spurious utterances which strengthened these convictions formed a pervasive web of falsehood which encouraged muddled thinking and superficial observation. It led to actions which were not based on a perception of religious and historical reality, and could therefore do nothing to heal the sickness at the core of the community.

Again, all of this is strikingly appropriate within the historical context to which Jeremiah addressed himself. The prophet stood on the brink of a vast crisis in the history of his nation, and we ought not be surprised if the internal disintegration which contributed so much to this crisis was viewed by him as equally broad in scope. Everything seemed to be working against the welfare of the nation, and he did all that was in his power to shatter the illusions of the people and arrest the destructive tendencies which he saw at work among them. That the great catastrophe came, that Jeremiah fades out of sight without having accomplished his purpose of averting it, is a tragedy for the people, the prophet, and for Yahweh as well (cf. Jer. 45). But it is a tragedy which reflects much more on the pervasive and destructive force of *šeqer* in the communal life than upon the quality of the prophet's insights or the diligence of his efforts.

The study which we have undertaken is now complete. It is hoped that in the process of examining in detail the central place which the concept *šeqer* plays in the message of Jeremiah some light has been shed on the concerns which motivated his activity and the way he gave them expression, as well as upon the underlying assumptions and convictions on which his utterances were based. It is hoped as well that in the course of the discussion some contribution may have been made to the understanding of certain perennial problems of Old Testament study, for example, the matter of 'false prophecy'.

INDEX OF AUTHORS

INDEX OF BIBLICAL REFERENCES